BodyHome

Literary Acknowledgements

Body is a Book is a Home, *Stone Highway Review*, May 2012
Diving In, *Eunoia Review*, April 2013
Objects of Desire, *THIS*, January 2012; *Red Fez*, August 2012
On Ecstasy, *Sleet*, Spring 2012
Linda, *Embodied Effigies*, March 2012
Coupons, *Free State Review*, Spring 2041
On Grief, *Flagler*, Spring 2012
Howls, *Owen Wister*, May 2014
Restricted, *Pithead Chapel*, May 2013
Vaginatarian, *Quaint*, August 2014
Matchbooks, Pennies, *The Meadow*, Summer 2014
Joe, *Twenty-four Hours*, March 2014
Your Lesbian Haircut, *Bookends*, January 2013
Hands, *SN Review*, Spring 2012
Sarah, *The Coachella Review*, January 2013
Seven, *The Dying Goose*, Spring 2013
Family Jewels, *Cliterature*, Spring 2014
What you Finally Attend To, *Cobalt*, March 2013
Curtains, *Seltzer*, April 2014
BodyHome, *Revolution House*, Spring 2012

BodyHome

Chelsey Clammer

Thank you
so much for
your support
and the good words
you put into the
world.
M—Sp

Hopewell Publications

BodyHome Copyright © 2015 by Chelsey Clammer.

Published by
Hopewell
Publications, LLC
PO Box 11,
Titusville, NJ 08560-
0011
(609) 818-1049

info@HopePubs.com
www.HopePubs.com

International Standard Book Number: 9781933435497

Library of Congress Control Number: 2014960073

First Edition

Printed in the United States of America

To Mindy for giving me life,
to Kristy and Marya for helping me learn how to live it.

Acknowledgements

Marya Hornbacher: this book wouldn't exist without you. Seriously. I hope you know that.

There are many years of my life that passed between experiencing my stories and publishing these essays. Expectantly, there are many people to thank who helped me to live, to write, to be inspired, to not give up, to make mistakes, to fix mistakes, to get up from falling down, to think through, to laugh, to feel loved, and to believe that *yes, I can do this*. So that covers everyone I have ever met.

More specifically:

This is where I thank my family—which consists of people with whom I share blood, as well as those friends who feel like family. Mindy Clammer, Kate Buley, Sabrina Long, Gma Hall, Pat Hall, Denna Clammer, Clayton Davis, Sarah Follmer, Beth Gerard, Ashley Johnson, Ruth Berger, Christi Furnas, Casey Heidiman, and Debbie McCulliss. And Jen, too—wherever you are.

This is where I thank my guides/mentors/bosses-turned-friends. Kristy Arditti, Rae Bryant, Linda Bubon, Ann Christophersen, Kathie Bergquist, Susan Post, and, of course, Brittany Fonte.

Also: a huge thanks to Julie Marie Wade for voluntarily reading the first complete draft of this book. Yikes.

Everyone at STAR, Rocky, and all of Urban Peak for simply existing. Hopewell Publications: you rock. A huge thank you to Lia Purpura and all those Rainier Writing Workshop folks for welcoming me into their tribe.

And Spencer. Thank you for helping me believe in not *if* but *when*.

Table of Contents

Body is a Book is a Home

Once upon a time there was a woman whose body was her home.

Inside her home were many books. Inside these books were many stories. Stories of the heart, collections of bones, the prose of blood. (Each book has a spine.) The woman whose body was a home collected those volumes and neatly lined them up along the shelves of her rib cage. When she breathed, pages fluttered and words coursed through her body. Letters escaped her lips.

Some of these stories were delightful little tales with promises of happy endings.

Some of them were dark mysteries—reaching their ends was always a difficult endeavor.

The woman whose body was a home made of books did not like thrillers very much, so she kept them tucked away. Every once in a while, one would fall from her ribs, ricochet down her spine, echo creeping along the structure of her skeleton. Reverberations rose inside her, split open her lips, pumped a screeching noise through her throat, the thrillers and mysteries then splayed open. They took up too much space.

After the screaming spell ceased, the woman would reorganize her books, bury the loud volumes deep inside, put the poetic ones on display. Her skin was a well-told story. She liked how words could swathe and how layers of stories shushed along her flesh each time she moved.

She held them all and gave each word a home. Close to her chest.

Diving In

1.

Winter. I've started smoking again, have somehow convinced myself to un-cozy this body from this apartment and into the 25-degree Chicago air. 4am. Grasping a mug of coffee. Smoking a cigarette. The form of my body slightly sways from side-to-side as I shift my weight from foot-to-foot, switching which slippered sole stands firm on the sidewalk. One shoulder settles, leans against the side of the building. It grounds me. One hand raises the cigarette to my lips. An inhale, an exhale. An inhale, an exhale, and I shove off the wall, switch the shoulder that grounds me, a subtle early morning dance I do to keep me warm until the cigarette is done. Then, upstairs to my apartment with a mug full of cold coffee.

There's an essay in which the narrator does what I'm doing. The ritual of smoking in the 4am quiet air that envelopes a dark street. I got the idea from those words, wanted to act out the narrator's actions. She made the image of an early morning outside cigarette in the cold sound soothing. I want to know that type of soothe, that type of serenity, and so I follow suit. This isn't about the narrator, but to engage in similar activities, to feel closer to the words, the writer I greatly admire as I do what she does. Feet shuffling, lungs inhaling, eyes that gaze at a silent street. It's something about being the only one awake. Smoking isn't a normal part of my life, but when I read delicious words of a woman having a 4am cigarette, instantly it integrates itself into my morning ritual. Because it feels right. Because it pulls my flesh closer to the words. Puffing into the shivering air and grabbing hold of the wispy thoughts that swirl like smoke up to the black sky, I sink my body into the memories of words, those elements of this world that keep me cozy, keep me breathing. Alive.

2.

Pages crackle as the covers bend in my hands. Poetry spills out, slips over my skin. The open spine releases words that nosedive through my flesh, plunge into the prose of my body. There is the smell of ink pressing into fingers, the oily feel of each letter that transfers from page to fingertip, staking a claim on identity. The page dampens as my fingers transfer their own oil back. Evidence of my reading infatuation left behind. Each page proof of being.

3.

My body leans into a bookcase. My eyes lean into the sight of a poet turning book into breath. In the back of this bookstore, on a short stage centered in the middle of the kid's book section, the bright covers of Curious George and Peter Rabbit sit behind her, listening. She speaks. Or reads, rather. No, more than that. More than just putting more words into the world. It's about her breath embodying language. Words that fill the air. Words that won't stay still. They travel to me, through me, greet me under my skin. This is a body full with sensation, soaking in the sound of beauty vocalized. Flesh, lungs, bones, blood—every facet of my anatomy listening to the rhythm of her language, the linguistics that glide from idea to meaning. The high tide of enticing words. My body becomes prose.

Here's why: The beat of her breath births each sentence into a sensation. Inflections make muscles flex. Words drum. A soothe and a sway. A lyric pulse that pushes and eases its way into me, into the space between each caesura she creates. The texture of prose. This is no longer simply listening. This is experiencing, connecting, becoming present in this attentive flesh. Existence thrums.

Narrative emerges from body.

4.

Night. Reading a book in bed. My fingers weave through the loom of my hair. The light brown dreadlocks that twist around my palms. Inside, a poem palpitates. Outside, a texture twirls. An encouraging touch—one that keeps my body here, aware, grounded so my brain can go there, into a different narrative. The feel of my hair, its hilly landscape coaxes me to be present in this body— even when my brain is attentive to another story. I am a novice at this activity, this keeping my body engaged while reading. Immersion occurs.

Though not always. When I read in the bath, the chair, or on the couch, there is physical loss in each tale, each stanza. I become a brain with no body, a reader with no physical feeling. Numb, almost. Diving into a book to get out of my body. The vulnerability of letting a story inside. This can be scary, though the sound of a poet reciting her lines jars my body alive, shows me how the body is a part of reading, that it's necessary, in fact, for this silent, solo activity to fully take a hold of me, to nudge me into a different understanding. A poet's embodied voice. And then a body that wants to be a part of the story. Every story and each letter that creates them. If I want words to live inside of me, then I must let them in, must dive flesh-first into them.

5.

Learning how to read is a matter of jumping into books.

Four years old. Bedroom floor. Lying on my stomach. Pages of a picture book splayed open. A captivating tale looking up. There's the desire to be in the book, really *in* it, wanting to play with those characters. Be a part of that story.

I hoist my body off the floor. Feet planted in the gray carpet, toeing the edge of the book, bending my knees deep, now spring. The dream of landing in the center of the story. My body lands on the pages, instead of travel-ing into them, like expected. I am not transported into the tale. Try again. Jump. Nothing. Jump. Nothing. Long, brown, four-year-old French braids hit the base of my neck with each bounce, each tip hitting back with proof of failure. But I want those braids to soar upwards as I fly down into the story's fantastic wonderland. Jump. Nothing. After a fifth attempt, I digress to stomping my foot on the book, frustrated that all of those characters in the marvelous little tale won't let me in. Why can't I be a part of the story? With more stomping, a page soon rips, the tale now ruined.

6.

At twenty-four, my knees are bent deep, my body squatting down low in an antiquarian bookstore. Three days ago the term "antiquarian" was not a part of my vocabulary. Old books were *rare*. Those dusty texts that didn't seem like anyone would consider them as treasures were never thought of as *antiquarian* in my mind. They were just obsolete tomes, words that lonely, withered old men hunted down in order to feel a connection with something as ancient as them. But now I squat, my body in a store with *antiquarian* in its name, looking for something archaic with which to connect. I'm not quite sure what, but something. Preferably by a woman.

Diane, a woman I don't personally know, prodded me in this direction. Diane is an author who created a character named Margaret. The novel is called *The Thirteenth Tale*, and in it, Margaret owns an antiquarian bookstore. Wanting to connect with Diane's fictional world and enticing words drove me to this real-life antiquarian bookstore.

Diane lured me with words about the smell and feel of old books stacked on shelves. Margaret, a book lover every book lover would love, ran her fingers along the dusty spines, and immediately my fingers wanted to also slide along old spines, my skin wanted to know old books, wanted to take into my body the palpitations of the text, of Margaret's movements. This is the sign of a well-written book, and so the search for something that will bring me closer to Margaret soon began.

Wanting to feel the events Margaret experienced, I gathered my thoughts and went to the antiquarian bookstore in the next town over. A long journey to quell a longing. Now, as I slowly rise from the bottom of the fiction shelf—the W's brought me no relief—my hands grasp the creaky wooden bookshelf to steady a head rush, a flash of red that sweeps through my body. Lately my diet has consisted solely of devouring Margaret's tale. So consumed with it, the thought of food has escaped me. Nibbling at and gnawing on this is what has sustained me. The story has expanded in my body. And as the Gothic tale came to a close, the need to inject an ancient copy of *Jane Eyre* into my veins, to feel a text as dark and eerie as *The Thirteenth Tale*, pulsated through me.

Once the head rush passes through, my eyesight un-reds, the A's becoming clear. *Jane Eyre* is not anywhere on the shelf, but *Ethan Frome* is. Grabbing it, there is the rush to the counter, the purchase, then the rush home to refill my body with the Gothic. *The Thirteenth Tale* sits on the shelf next to me as I engulf *Ethan Frome*, its pages soon dwindling in my hands, story now also stored in my body. Margaret's adventure, her body in motion as she stumbled around a crumbling house in order to solve the mysterious plot, sits on the shelf of my bones, on the rungs of my rib cage as more stories seep into my blood. Margaret's final gasps collected at the bottoms of my lungs, my toes became blue with cold as the phantasmal night fell upon her narrative. My body remembers these things as a similar story enters my skin. Once the pages of *Ethan Frome* are put to rest, the feeling of another Gothic tale fully nestles into the cavity of my chest.

7.

The book will end, but my body will forever want more. A good story never completely satisfies; it leaves one wanting. A good book teases. When presented with such a satisfying text, every bit of it is consumed in one day, except for those last twenty pages. Those final pages are a delicate dessert; the story's end is meant to be savored. Covet those final words like a secret stash. Anxiety over the book's end rises, but is quelled if you let a morsel of the text remain while you find your next fix— the next tantalizing collection of gratifying words. It will take another week to finish those last twenty pages, not for a lack of interest, but out of a need to keep the characters' lives alive, breathing through the letters ballooning from the page and into your eyes. There will always be more craving for such a satisfying story, so weaning the body off of it slowly is the only safe way to end the relationship.

Nearing the final pages, my grip on the book tightens. They are about to take flight, their departure something I try to deny.

But when the end comes, my body cuddles with the story one last time. Falling asleep with her in my arms, the last breath of our relationship exhaled, I will wake up to face the next few days it will take to fully let her go, to really be able to immerse myself in another book.

A way to transition through this twinge of grief, to re-center myself, is through engaging in a favorite activity: used bookstore browsing. There's the longing, the hunt, and the satisfaction. There's the discovery of something that didn't know it needed to be found. Finding it is ecstasy. How a sense of calm sweeps through my body even now, even as all I am doing is remembering moments when a book surprised me with its existence—a book that spoke to a buried part of me that needed to be spoken to, a reality that has yet to be realized.

On the rare occasion when a trip to the used bookstore results in no real find, my bookshelves are there to offer suggestions for what will fill the parts of me that yearn to feel complete. The effects of a reading obsession would probably be eased if books were not a hoarded thing. But they are not eased. And while the compulsion to share beloved texts with the beloved people in my life is always present, lending a treasured text, relinquishing what's cherished from its home on dependable shelves is not something one should do, because once released, the book might never come back. Just expect this. And please, learn from my mistakes and never do this. Too many books that formed my identity have been lost to ex-lovers. Do not go down that haunted road. Because that's exactly how it feels when a book becomes permanently gone. Its ghost lingers nearby. Its empty place on the shelf feels dark, cold. Gaping. An unnerving tinge of sadness creeps beneath skin with the realization of what's lost. Such grief.

8.

There is reading, and then there is experiencing. There is understanding a story, and then there are the ways in which words can hold up a mirror. Letters create a reflection. Words imprint on veins long before the author feels them in her own hands. Reading these books to know their stories is unnecessary. It's about being a reader who could have written those words herself. It's about reading ten pages, then waiting a few weeks to read another ten—the space between not a break as the story acts itself out every day. Daily, words multiply, spread throughout the knowing body. An obsession begins. The book consumes each thought. The reader's life lives the text. There is no need to read the book. It's in you.

9.

My body has always, will always, inhabit each text that enters my life. Yes, the act of reading resides in the mind, but the body *experiences* language. From this, one can never completely separate oneself from those words. The text is there, forever palpating. Through emulation and inundation, through the dream of jumping into books, through taking trips to antiquarian bookstores, used bookstores, it is with each word ingested, each sentence, that coaxes one to further sink into skin, body.

Objects of Desire

A mug full of homemade sangria sat in the cup holder between us, nestled next to the console. Bits of apple bobbed in the blood red liquid, as Rose did not avoid the pot holes.

"Did she fist you, too?" Rose asked, both hands on the steering wheel.

My fingers held on tight to a cigarette as my arm dangled outside the passenger side window, playing with the air whooshing by. I gripped the mug of sangria, and chugged. "Dude," I said after a moment's pause, "she plunged into me without asking."

"Oh me gawd!" Rose squealed in her east coast accent; the accelerator pushed a bit harder. "The girl made me bleed!"

"Me too!" I gleefully shouted, a bit relieved.

But this is not where the story begins.

It starts with my second grade teacher, Ms. Gray, not a hottie, but crush-worthy. She was sexy in the sense that I wanted to be engulfed by her, by her strong mountain arms. Wanted her to love me like a mother, because what other type of love is there? And yeah, I was seven and confusing maternal love with crushed-out-on-my-teacher love. (Authority figures do it for me.) Not so weird. The "learn about sex" book my mother would give me to read in fifth grade said so. Crushes on older females were okay.

So was sex among black people, or people in wheelchairs. Cartoons of diversity doing it. The book didn't discriminate against desire.

Now, lying in bed, my hand deciding which large chunk of silicone is the correct width for this anticipated moment in time, I realize my crush on Ms. Gray is also not where this story begins. It actually begins with a candle. Another crush, although this time on a boy. Weird. I blame curiosity. Eighth grade: Some of my friends were already having sex. A girl who was not my friend was pregnant. Proof of her curiosity expanding in her body. My curiosity led to a candle. Once inside, there was no flame of desire rising. No swelling heat for the boy who was not physically there with me and the candle, even though images of him were trying to insert themselves in my mind. Nope. Didn't work. What boredom.

Penetration was yawn-worthy.

Penetration was pointless.

And yet.

Now, lying in bed, back propped up on three brown pillows, the decision as to which of the three large dildos will be used tonight is feeling harder than it should be. A bit tired, I know I only have one orgasm in me. So. A blue sphinx, a silver dolphin, or a pink rabbit?

But before now, I'm twenty-two and at the supermarket buying cucumbers and condoms. I feel obvious. This, however, is cheaper and somehow less embarrassing than buying a vibrator. I put a packet of gum on the conveyer belt to hopefully distract the cashier from smirking. Wait. No. Taking a pause from trying to figure out which vibrator I want to use tonight (sphinx vs dolphin vs rabbit), I light a cigarette and remember it wasn't cucumbers, but zucchini. The cucumbers looked too big. The zucchini were curved. That sounded something like pleasure.

A great line from a woman in a feminist porn writing workshop around the time of the zucchini: "It was like throwing a hot dog down a hallway." This does not apply to me and the zucchini.

Accoutrements used in attempts to get off:

- Jumbo-sized black Sharpee
- Jumbo-sized black Sharpee with toilet paper taped to the end of it for padding (lesson learned from the first go-round)
- Brush handle
- Family dog's tongue (bestiality never developed)
- Aforementioned candle (peach)
- Pencil (hot dog in a hallway)
- Beer bottle (unwanted foreign object inserted by first girlfriend in a hot tub)

Here is where I circle back to the story of Kristin's fist, which, in a way, was a foreign object. No time for preparation, that alien fist was momentarily unwanted. Her fist, an object of desire, new to me. Once inside, good god I loved it, wanted more of it, more of her in me: Fuck yeah, please find that spot, that spot I want to find tonight. Back then, her big fist filled me as desire punched around my inner cavity. (force = mass x acceleration). Now, a decision needs to be made. Like, seriously, *right now*. The sphinx is the skinniest of the three; its mass is now dismissed.

Three years after the zucchini, my current lover and I discuss the concept of fisting. She has never been fisted. I have never slept with a man. The conversation is not erotic, but technical. (We find we have much in common.) The two acts are not comparable, unless it's one damn big penis. She doesn't understand how a fist does not feel like a punch. *Depends on the force of the fist. Also, the hand enters not in a fist, but once inside, the fist is made. Then the game is on.*

"Did you ever read *Where the Red Fern Grows?*" I ask.

"Uh. Yeah."

"Remember the raccoon trap? There's the shiny object at the bottom of the trap. The raccoon has to slide his hand into a small hole to get to it, but he can't pull it out of the trap with the object he desires gripped in his hand. His fist is too big, and his hand gets stuck. Which means his body is stuck, pumping around inside the trap."

G-spot goes a-tingle. Erogenous zone aroused. Hours of sex. My "learn about sex" book didn't explain how to feel around for the g-spot, the rough, bean-shaped patch of nerves found hanging out on the wall somewhere back there.

Me, well I'm more of a clit person. Though, female ejaculation is always fun. Neither my current lover nor I have squirted with anyone but ourselves. She shows me her Hitachi wand. I tell her I like dual action. (It's our differences we share.)

Now, the cigarette is put out, and the wondering continues. Silver dolphin or pink rabbit? Which type of animality does my body want to feel tonight? (Answer = Mine)

The jumbo-sized Sharpee made me bleed. Kristin and her fist made me bleed. I jerked off yesterday, my menstrual cycle in full swing. Shark Week, my friends call it. The first time my new lover and I had sex, she took her tampon out in the bathroom before we started (nothing comes between us). She tasted metallic. Soft iron.

Julie surprised me with her tampon, surprised me by bringing out the toys on our first of only two fuckings (too much between us). She was the tennis coach at my high school. (Authority figures do it for me.)

Gloria Anzaldua: "Escribo con la tinta de mi sangre."

I used to only write with a red pen, to see me, my blood on paper. To put all of me in my writing. Now, it's blue. My veins visible on the page. Tap into it. Get it all out. Let it hang in the air, then descend onto the page. Write with legs spread open.

Legs crossed, reading. Mall: Tracy, California, circa 1996. My mother and I go into Walden Books. She buys me the Dean Koontz novel I didn't get to finish reading as it was due back to the library the day before. My mother encourages me to read, explore. Grabbing the purchased book from her, telling her I absolutely have to finish the chapter *now*, she admires my enthusiasm for words. Prancing to a bench, my mother watches as I open the book right in the middle of it as if this was exactly where I left off. This is a lie. Mom's eyes turn around, stare elsewhere. Fingers then flip through the pages to get to *the scene.* Desperately. Young girls and their hormones. On the bench in the middle of the mall, legs crossed and squished together, the position squeezes me in just the right spot. Florescent lights yellow the page (283). Mom wanders off. And there it is: The sex scene starring Elisabeth's creamy skin. Legs together, tighter. A few days later, not a few re-readings, but dozens, the passage is easily memorized. Words living in my skin. (Ecstasy burns through the brain.) At the mall, reading and re-reading the same page until my mother returns, bored, my underwear have become vaguely moist (not bored). Such a voracious reader.

Once, my belly was smashed against the rubber padding of a weight lifting machine at my gym. Lifting seventy pounds with my ankles and pulling the weight toward my ass, my legs squeezed together, tight. Tighter. And then, well hello there—a surprise orgasm that shivered through my body (Lifetime Fitness). After the orgasm interruption, men began to grunt in the free weights area.

Men's asses aren't attractive. They do not sway like a good ass should sway. Female muscular arms are attractive. I have always wanted them.

Cross country practice, freshman year of high school. One runner talks amongst the team about how she hates running with a pad on. "Feels like a full diaper about to fall." Our coach (female) tells her to use a tampon. Reagan says she can never insert it all the way. "Honey, just think of Eric when you put it in."

Regan has perfect, sexy, female muscular arms.

Kate Bornstein: "Don't be anyone you wouldn't want to fuck. Don't fuck anyone you wouldn't want to be."

Dolphins have orgasms.

My decision sways.

Kristin had great taste in books. She was a voracious reader. I lent her a book about a young lesbian in India. She later lent the book to Rose, who was also a voracious reader (desire shared). Rose's ass swayed like a good ass should. The questioning continues. Dolphin or rabbit. Consider the dolphin, consider its mass, and consider the type of orgasm that will quickly be had. Perhaps implement isn't important, because thoughts of a good ass swaying like a good ass should sway (Rose) make me not need much to get off. Decide. Insert. Buzz. BAM!

Kristin's arms were not muscular, but strong. Mountain strong. Frida Kahlo on her right arm (art in motion).

Only straight erotica gets me wet. My attempts at writing straight erotica in a feminist porn writing workshop were lame. Boring. Like how I imagine straight sex must be. (I'm a clit person.) The feminist porn workshop leader was also a yoga teacher. Thus, yoga poses to start off each class. Downward dog will forever get me ready. But it will not prepare me for writing about what I don't know. Which is why my straight erotica always sounded so fake. (Fiction is not my style.) Eventually, my writing swung back to my sexuality and led to an essay about eating a doughnut off a woman's crotch (jeans on) in front of a movie theater crowd.

Experience check-in:

Food consumed during sex:

- Strawberries
- Whipped Cream

Adventurous food isn't for me.

Handmade shirt worn to shreds in college read "vaginatarian."

High school. First girlfriend. She was a cowgirl. She didn't have rope when we tried bondage. We used my mother's green elastic exercise bands. My body failed at staying still as the bands stretched too much (the necessity of tough resistance).

A line I wrote in my feminist porn writing workshop:

"I get wet. Real wet. When having sex in a hot tub, I raise the water level." (Memoir is my style.)

Kristin made me wet, wet with blood, wet with a surprise fist as she wouldn't drop the shiny object of her desire, my desire.

The dolphin is shiny (silver). The rabbit is shiny (pink). My desire is shiny (wet). My decision is coming.

Seventeen. Locked in the bathroom stall of a Souper Salad! with the cowgirl. (Taste in food attempting to be adventurous.) Hopes of attending to my vaguely moist underwear led us here.

Twenty. In the supermarket with my second girlfriend. She sees an eggplant and exclaims, "I've always wanted to have an eggplant *and* a girlfriend!" See: Dorothy Allison's short essay "The Lesbian Appetite." Sex with eggplants. This girlfriend had a great taste (in words, too).

We bought each other eggplant necklaces. We never had sex with an eggplant. (Words stay on the page.)

Souper Salad! does not serve eggplant.

Richard was fifty and only had eight fingers. He said two were bitten off by a shark. (Fictional appetites are not my style.) I was fucking his girlfriend, Carrie. Carrie was married, had a girlfriend, a boyfriend with eight fingers, and a son as old as me. I met Carrie in a psych ward. She got kicked out for cuddling with me in my bed. I was there because my mind was missing its serotonin. (Ecstasy burns through the brain.)

a) Sex on ecstasy: boring
   a. Jerking off while on ecstasy: not boring
b) Justification: I ended up humping the blue carpet of my grandfather's mountain cabin.
c) Caution: Orgasm cannot occur while drunk.
   a. (present tense is more my style)
d) Caution: Having an orgasm while stoned is an oxymoron.
   a. (tensed muscles are more my style)

Once, I let a dude believe I would fuck him in exchange for cocaine. He left some coke cut into nice lines sitting on the bathroom counter. He went into the bedroom. My best friend and I did lines in his bathroom. I took his pocket knife from the counter and slid it into my pocket. One more sniff each and the we ran out of there, laughing maniacally.

Once, after we did coke in a bathroom stall, my boss kissed me. (Authority figures do it for me.) She played the part of an organization's president. My part was publicist. She organized events. She brought the coke. I forget what her boyfriend did for a living.

I never actually had sex in a Souper Salad! bathroom stall. The cowgirl and I only made out. Before we could get our clothes off, two soccer moms walked in with three daughters. One stall (occupied), and the girls had to pee, real bad. Impatience pressing on their bladders. They asked what was taking so long. Cowgirl finally opened the stall door (peach). Eyes averted, we left the bathroom, heads down, avoiding motherly smirks. Tight cowgirl Wranglers pressed against the proof that she is a woman, even though her shaved head made everyone assume that "he" was in the wrong bathroom. The soccer moms took note of her breasts.

A queen-sized bed is, in fact, big enough for five women.

An organic farmer with a song for every vegetable melted my vibrator. A pussy does, in fact, get hot. So does boiling a vibrator in water for the purpose of sanitation. (The dual-action butterfly did not live long enough to make it to tonight's competition. RIP, you fine lady.) The organic farmer taught me which flowers are edible (adventurous food). Nasturtium. I never slept with her. She never paid me back for the vibrator.

At 4am, I'm in my roommate's office, talking with her about writing. One of her dachshunds ("douche-hound" not the correct pronunciation, as I had believed until a few months ago when a friend corrected me) trots into the room and drops my vibrator on the hardwood floor, looking satisfied. Plunk. At 4am, I'm in my roommate's office, looking along with her at the pink vibrator. Too sleepy to care about embarrassment, I instead grab the silicone pink rabbit and say thank you (sanitation now necessary).

Back to being seventeen: My dog is whining from the kennel near my foot. The cowgirl and I are fucking on the hardwood floor. When my mother knocks on the locked bedroom door inquiring what all of the noise is about, specifically what we are doing, I open it, and unthinkingly wipe my chin while saying, "Oh, just hanging out."

My fourth girlfriend and I smeared red edible body paint in swirling designs around our nipples. As we licked our bodies clean, we broke our vegan diets. (Insects sacrificed themselves for red dye—red desire.)

I have always wondered if lesbians could actually claim to be vegans. We eat each other's animality. (Beastiality never developed.)

A shirt worn in grad school said: "Eat me, I'm organic."

Words have always turned me on.

To this day, I do not know how to pronounce cunni-lingus. To this day, I have to Google it to find out how to spell it. Dictionaries fail the English language. The tongue gets all twisted up with this word, with the actions of this word.

I have always thought "linguistics" sounded sexual. The study of human speech, and, essentially, the tongue forming words. To like licking language.

When I got bored waiting for the cowgirl to come, I spelled out the alphabet with my tongue on her clit. I got her started, precision in its straighforwardness. She always came around S. I only made it to Z once. It was the most fun letter to form. The sideways flicker of a tongue (gears shifting).

Now, I shift the brown pillows behind my back, and reach for the lube (colorless, but shiny, obviously). I think about the cowgirl, then shift memories to that of Kristen, to the feel of her fist pounding in me. (Acceleration is a change in velocity over a change in time; $a = Dv/Dt$.) I consider the equation of that impact, the impact that impacted my current concept of desire. My brown dread-locks sweep across my pink, puckered nipples as I settle in with, or rather sit on top of, the dolphin (silver).

My third girlfriend said she thought my dreads looked like little penises. She thought they felt like ropes. She made me pull them back when we had sex. (The current lover pulls them.) What's wrong with rope? It's better than an exercise band. She was a bore in bed. Claimed to have lockjaw syndrome, and thus couldn't go down on me. And for six months, claimed to have a yeast infection, and thus I couldn't go down on her. I bought "us" a vibrator (pink rabbit). I bought it for me. She never used it. Yesterday, it was covered in blood (Shark Week). Today, a dachshund delivered it. (Sanitation performed this morning.)

If a bulimic woman fingerbangs a woman with a yeast infection, then later, with unwashed hands, makes herself puke, can she get a yeast infection in her throat? (Desire expanding.)

My favorite word in the English language is "bangover."

I have injured myself many times while masturbating.

Injuries:

- chafing
- IT Band syndrome (overused, tight hips)
- numb feet (not an injury, but still painful)
- assortment of bruises (the arm of the chair is not padded well)
- wall burn on elbow
- punctured bean-shape place of nerves on the wall somewhere back there (unpadded Jumbo-sized black Sharpee (lesson learned))

Once, I had sex with a woman named Kat in an alley. My back scraped against the brick wall of a dingy bar, her bent knees banged against two dumpsters. Yes, sex in an alley with a creature named Kat. I never called her my alleycat. (Beastiality never developed.)

The cowgirl had a big truck. On the tailgate was a slur of bumper stickers. Specifically: "Save a horse, ride a cowboy."

Different car. This one, a red convertible. Driver: blonde soccer mom type. Bumper sticker in tiny font: "If you're going to ride my ass that hard, you might as well pull my hair."

The girlfriend who thought my hair was like ropes but never pulled it had her nose pierced. She would kiss my forehead, and my hair would get stuck in the white stud. We never spent time figuring out if my pubic hair could get snagged on the stud. (Oh that damn "Lock Jaw.") Imagine the feel of pulled pubic hair.

Pulling on my armpit hair makes the backs of my legs tingle.

I pull on my armpit hair before popping open the lube and putting it to use.

This story really begins with my parents' bedroom. It's where my mom told me about sex. It's where, when she told me that "penis + vagina = sex," I thought of Steve Urkel from "Family Matters." Thought of Urkel and his neighbor, Lisa, lying in bed together, flat on their backs, a quilt covering their young bodies as some tube of his penis was inside her. The lack of movement. Lisa asks if the sex is over yet. (I have always had a hard time with geometry.)

If *a* intersects with *b* at point *x*, there must be something worthy of *why?*

I push the brown pillows away and think more of a good ass swaying. Kristen pushed that desire into me, pushed at that previously unknown desire for something pushed into me. I think of Kristen's Frida Kahlo in motion with each pump.

On the subject of pornography: I have never enjoyed faking it.

On the subject of faking it: My throat feels scratchy when I breathe in and out too roughly. (She never liked the feel of my rough, ropey hair. My throat often felt rough around her.)

My head feels light when I'm faking it.

Kristin made me feel grounded, pounded.

And while we shared similar fisting experiences, Rose and I never fucked, never faked it with each other. In her car, I chugged the last of the sangria and thought about how her ass sways like a good ass should. (The story begins.)

The dolphin sways. (Desire expands.)

On Ecstasy

The green lighter's wheel grinds back with the force of my father's thumb. It's a smashed thumb, a thumb he hit with a hammer years ago, years before the idea of me was even conceived. The wheel turns. Fire sparks. Dad's deep chocolate eyes stand out, are illuminated by the flame waving inches away from this face. Cigarette lit, the low-grade flash of fire quits. The man standing before me becomes a blur as he is engulfed by the night, by that crisp darkness that will give space for the shape of a conversation that's about to occur, to let it grow.

But first, a few moments before, minutes past midnight. I wake my father up and plead for him to come join me for a midnight cigarette. An odd act. Odd since I rarely talk to him. Odd since he has no idea I smoke. Though there's not a hint of hesitation in his movements. Untangling his ungainly body from a bed full of sheets twisted around his legs, he agrees to my proposition of a smoke. He grabs his pack, takes two out. Elated, I skip down the hall and to the front door. It's the ecstasy in my blood that propels me, launches me along.

Now into the night air. Thighs swishing against skirt swishing against thighs. Tactility waves hello to itself. My skin tingles, stars vibrate in the sky above me. This is what love must feel like—that full body that's full of electricity, sparks and shimmering, blasts of excitement. A full body that's full of ecstasy. Even my toes, even my tongue all hum right along to the tune of those ecstatic *fuck yeah!* chimes dancing in my eardrums. Euphoria whistling. Thank you, ecstasy. All of me, all of my body zaps into the air as I twirl around to face my father. His face speaks a collection of thoughts—thoughts that the ecstasy which courses loudly through my veins, my brain, keeps me from hearing. Though it appears he doesn't care that his youngest daughter is rolling hard right in front of him. Because drugs or not, here's the daughter who despises him now wanting to smoke a father-daughter cigarette.

This is me: Eighteen. High on ecstasy. Outside, under huge plops of stars, standing next to the large oak tree in front of our Austin home. My dad's cigarette sizzles with satisfaction. An item being put to use. I am on ecstasy for the fourth night in a row. My friends burnt out after the third night, but I'm persistent, tenacious, and I stubbornly refuse to stop doing the drug. I don't want to take a hiatus from this high. I don't feel the drug burning holes in my brain, not yet, though it will in a few days. Instead of pain, what I feel in this precise moment of a smoke being lit is satisfied from witnessing a cigarette's stellar performance, how it perfectly conveys what a job well done can look like. My dad hands over a Marlboro Ultra Light 100 and the green lighter. Smoke lit, I linguistically surge through something that's been bothering me lately, *quick*, before an awkward silence can settle in between us. Here it comes:

"So Courtney's pissing me off because she has this crush on another girl—my best friend Sabrina's girlfriend

Lee, actually—and she keeps telling me about how cute she thinks Lee is because it's better to talk about these things than to lie about them because that's how we have open communication and isn't that what a good relationship should have but I'd rather have her lie about Lee because I don't want to hear about her attraction to other women." I pause, inhale. Then exhale this confession: "It makes me feel ugly." Piercing the humid, summer air with my cigarette as I make this last statement, I then take a long drag and let my father tell me the things I need to hear most.

"Well, Chels," he begins, not skipping a beat to respond to my ecstasy-fueled diatribe. The drugs do not delude me. I can sense his utter confusion, how he's taken aback by the absurdity of this situation. I've been an out and proud lesbian for two years now, but my dad and I have never discussed the fact of my queer sexual orientation. We just don't connect like that, just don't know how to talk about anything besides the truck he bought me or the computer he bought me or the stereo he bought me. But in this moment, in these first few seconds of his fatherly response starting to seep out, I see a different dad, one who cares about—perhaps even loves—his youngest daughter. Through the manic shrieks of ecstasy, I devour the good and supportive energy that's here now, twirling around with the nicotine traces of our steady breaths. He continues, gives me stellar advice. Here it comes:

Advice. Advice. Advice. Advice. Advice.

I have no idea what he says.

Again, the drugs.

But it's the feel of his voice, deep and smooth, that will stick to my mind, stick inside me way after he dislodges himself from this world. Now, his words glitter and glow through my skin. That permeable organ, a part of me finally letting a part of him in. A thing I've never before done, and I can feel the fact of it conga up and down my back. Those father eyes taking me in, his unspoken curiosities ladder along my skeleton. Steps now being taken to take our relationship into a space where it can thrive. Deepen. Vibe. Vibrations of his breath swirling around my flesh. Here is my dad, speaking to me for the first time like a dad speaks to his daughter. This is what love must feel like—that full body that's full of electricity, sparks and shimmering, blasts of excitement. Hello, my smile. Hello, brilliant lightning heating up between us, encouraging common feelings of adoration. My skin tingles. Emotions shimmer.

He talks to me, says whatever it is he says to help calm what small bit of my intoxicated and hyped-up nerves can be quieted. Quelled. The cigarette. His voice trails off with his smoke's end, but not before I can feel this tenuous something new between us visit me, see me through, see through me. And not before I understand that even a voice full of gibberish can taste just as sweet as nicotine on ecstasy.

Linda

An old schizophrenic woman sits in the courtyard at my work. Skinny legs cross over themselves, her body hunches forward in the green plastic chair. No one else sits in this chair. The other residents know it is her favorite spot, and they do not want to make her angry. She has an explosive temper. She screams into the night air about sins against God, about rape and whores and stealing.

She calls the Holy Ghost, "Casper." And she talks with God.

Her name is Linda. Her eyes are wide and milky, two blue-gray, oblong orbs that stare at the world intensely.

Coworkers warned me about this woman on my first day here. My supervisor told me Linda can be difficult, will call me a whore, will scream to me how I've sinned against her God. Another warning: She often refuses to take her meds. Towards the end of my first day of work— a tiring shift full of shadowing my supervisor, watching how he hands out meds to residents, how he logs this in the MAR—the old schizophrenic woman shuffled in, sat down, stared at him. She didn't notice me in the room, or if she did, she paid no attention to this new employee. My supervisor popped a mountain of meds out of their bubble packets and placed them in a paper cup. He handed the colorful assortment of tabs and capsules over to Linda, gave her another small cup—this one full of water—and didn't speak while she slipped each orange, yellow and white pill into her mouth, swallowed them with a small sip of water.

She spoke of her dreams between each swig.

The whore tried to kill me, honey, but I wouldn't let the devil spit his fire. God came to me, honey. God said you have to repent or you'll burn for your sins, honey. She filled each place where there could have been a pause with a stressed "honey." This changed something for me, made me see something that my coworkers must not have seen—how an angry woman could combine admonishments with endearments, could turn a threat into a warning with just one word. Meds ingested, she did not leave, but continued on about how God will punish us for our sins.

"Honey!" she screamed in her voice full of crushed gravel, the warning gaining intensity. "Listen to me. You have to repent to God, or you will die. REPENT TO GOD!" She screamed with eyeballs shaking.

Thrown back into my flesh by her screaming, scared that she would begin to yell at me, my body stayed still, tried to fade into the gray wall behind me. The supervisor just nodded at the outburst, hummed a little in agreement. After a beat of unfilled silence, Linda slowly rose, pushed herself out of the maroon, plastic chair with her hands on the desk that separated employees from residents. She walked out the door, threw words over her shoulder. "REPENT!" The screams continued down the hall, echoes following her into the courtyard. She sat in her chair.

Two weeks have passed since that day, and while there was that *honey* glimpse of how something in her might one day shift, she still makes my muscles tighten each time she enters the office. Trying to act relaxed around her to hide the anxiety her voice induces in me, I fight to keep my hands steady when I dispense her meds. But my coworkers continue to keep me stressed about Linda's presence.

Every day during changeover, we check in about how the day has so far been. Which clients had appointments, which ones had a new med to take. Each meeting ends with the question, *How's Linda today?* We sit in a circle on chairs and couches and stare at one another, passing information back and forth. The nurse said she's not doing well, that she's been screaming all day in the courtyard. The counselor says she refused to take her meds that morning. She's not doing well. This is not unusual.

The check-ins make me nervous about how my med pass will go that night when I'll have to find Linda to tell her to come and take her meds. She usually doesn't come down for them, and so I'm forced into the task of finding her, disrupting whatever conversation she's having with God in the courtyard. Though sometimes she's sitting in the cafeteria, alone, in the dark. Sometimes she's in her room. Like tonight. No one can go into her room. My coworkers warned me about this, told me she will scream at me to get out if I take one tiny step into her room.

My knuckles quietly tap three times on her door.

I speak to her in a way that reflects her words, hoping she will cooperate with a soft-spoken request.

"Honey?" Tap tap tap. No response. "Honey?" A bit louder.

"Yeah?" A graveled voice responds.

"Honey, do you want to come take your meds?"

"In a minute, honey." This means nothing. An hour will pass and she still won't appear. An hour will pass and light taps on her door will reoccur.

"Okay, honey." I walk away from her room, thankful this interaction didn't become an incident.

During my first week of training, she barely acknowledged my presence, that a new person was pushing a full cup of meds across the desk to her. She took the pills without speaking to me, looked lost in her own world, her body running on auto-pilot with a mind wandering off.

But after that first week, Linda started to recognize me, or at least started to look at me, blankly. She didn't speak, thankfully hadn't yet yelled, but her cracked voice traveled into my office late at night as she sat in the courtyard, screaming into the frosty January dark. I did not quite know how to navigate her screeches, her temper, so I made no command to quiet down.

A few weeks go by and she starts to show trust in me, or at least she's not irritated by me. She has yet to yell directly at me. Instead, she'll scream in my presence about doctors who are out to kill her. "What do you need, Linda?" A question to ask instead of trying to quiet her down like my coworkers do with demands to stop yelling. She doesn't like them. In fact, she screams louder at them when they tell her to stop screaming.

My approach to Linda is different. Let her talk; let her yell. Don't fight with her; don't tell her to quiet down. Other residents will complain that she's getting out of hand and something needs to be done about this. I don't do anything about this—just let her be. Linda eventually calms down. This approach has so far saved me from being called a whore. Disregarding how to do my job correctly by not letting her rant and disrupt the other residents, her screams will eventually calm down, her voice will eventually lower to a harsh whisper. When this occurs, everyone breathes a bit easier.

Tonight, an hour after my three soft taps on Linda's door asking for her to get her meds, she is still not here. Another trip up the stairs to Linda's room to encourage her to come out with another three knocks. She says nothing.

"Honey?"

She says nothing.

"Honey?"

She says nothing.

Then I do what I have been instructed to do when a resident will not come down for meds. Taking my master key, I unlock her door and walk in. This is risky, as with each entrance Linda will assume staff is stealing things from her, will disrupt her possessions. We do not steal her things. She's just so lost in her mind that she never remembers where she puts her keys, her favorite brown hoodie, her underwear. Regardless of possible accusations, Linda needs her meds, and it's my job to make sure she gets them. Taking my chances, my feet enter into her room. There is a dim lamp on; the pale pink lamp shade filters light throughout the room. Clean, folded clothes are in neat stacks on her large, wooden floor. She does laundry every day, fulfilling her need to stay clean, pure.

"Honey?" My voice whispers, again.

A small lump of a sleeping Linda lies on the bed.

"Honey, do you want to come take your meds?"

Staying in her bed, her face smashed into the pillow, Linda calmly says, "In a minute, honey."

Shouldn't she be yelling?

"Okay," I say, grateful for whatever god might be looking out for me. Back downstairs, just a few minutes go by and then she's shuffling into my office.

After the nightly routine of ingesting her mountain of meds, she says, "Honey, can I have a cigarette?" We're not supposed to do this. Workers are told on their first day to not give anything to the residents. It's about boundaries. But Linda needs a cigarette, will feel better once she smokes it, and it will stave off her yells for just a few moments. Doing more disregarding of the agency's rules, I reach into my coat pocket, pull out my pack of Camel Lights and hand her two.

"Oh, honey. Thank you."

Her eyes widen with her voice. She takes the cigarettes. She stands up.

"You know what you are, honey?"

"What's that, Linda?"

"You're an angel from God, honey." Her head nods at me as she exits out of the office repeating, "An angel from God." Linda goes into the courtyard, sits in her chair.

About bending the rules: In regards to Linda, we all do this. Though we only have to bend them at the end of the month. The residents get a meager stipend of $93 every thirty days, and by the last week, Linda runs out of money. This is a terrible situation. Linda believes that cigarettes help to calm down the symptoms of schizophrenia. No one knows if this is true, but what we do know is that it works with her. Perhaps there are some truths she knows. Though Linda also believes cigarettes are not addictive if you keep switching brands. Either way, she's calmer, happier when she has her cigarettes. At the beginning of each month, when she has plenty of smokes, Linda talks to other residents, hugs them, even, and they cheerfully respond to her, appreciative of the fact that she's in a good mood. Her cigarettes are really flavored cigars. All of the residents smoke these as they are only $1.50 a pack at the corner store down the street. I tried them once to see what it was they were smoking. They were absolutely disgusting. Strawberry flavored tobacco. Chocolate. Vanilla, too.

Cherry is Linda's favorite, though she puffs at these cigars without really smoking them. She sucks at the tip of them quickly, makes a sharp popping noise with her mouth, then immediately exhales the smoke. The nicotine probably doesn't even enter her body. But she's convinced they help her with her mental illness, so no one says anything, and we buy her cigarettes when she runs out, then leave her alone as she puff-pops away.

The other residents aren't jealous that we buy cigarettes for Linda, but not for them. Instead, they are thankful that we help to keep Linda calm.

A month after Linda finally starts to see me, she begins to motion for me to stand near her every time I walk through the courtyard.

"Honey. You work too hard. Come here, honey. Have a cigarette."

I start to join her in the courtyard for my cigarette breaks. She's nice to me, welcomes me to stand next to her as she tells me about the orphanage she grew up in because her mother was a whore and accidentally got pregnant with her and didn't want the burden of taking care of her. She tells me about the doctor who didn't attend to a patient in the nursing home she used to live in, which caused one of her friends to die. Women are whores. And doctors kill.

It doesn't matter if any of this is true, because she believes it is. The more Linda speaks with me, the more her rants start to make sense. A real feeling of unjustified and harmful actions committed against Linda, including a rape, boils within her, fuels her screams. I sympathize with her, believe that, while she may be diagnosed with schizophrenia, she has had a hard life, which brings on her screams.

Another month passes by, and Linda and I continue to grow closer to each other. The other residents don't understand this. They are shocked by how I got Linda to not only trust me, but to like me. From this weird sort of friendship that grows, I start to understand her more, start to know her routines. How she goes to the Dollar Store down the street and buys cleaning products and cans of beans. She shows them to me and says, "Honey, you have to go to the Dollar Store. It's at 18th and Nicollette, honey. Look at these beans. A dollar, honey. A *dollar*." She slowly shakes her head up and down and presses her lips together, widening her eyes into mine. "A *dollar*, honey." I tell her that's a great idea and I'll go to the Dollar Store tomorrow, even though I know I won't. She also goes to the church down the street at night and the nuns give her free items—boxes of Jello-O, sweatshirts, and other items donated by the community.

It's March now. Four months after my start date, Linda now comes down for her meds without needing me to prompt her.

"Oh, honey," her graveled voice begins. "I have something for you."

She's wearing her brown hoodie, as always, the hood tied tight around her head. She reaches into her pocket and pulls out a scratched tube of lipstick—obviously used.

"I got it for you at the church, honey. You are so beautiful. You deserve this."

"Oh, honey, that is so kind! Thank you, honey." I repeat her words, and maybe one of the reasons why she likes me is because of this. Knowing I'll never wear this used lipstick, will actually throw it away once she leaves, I say thank you and give her a warm smile.

"Put it on, honey. Let's see how beautiful you are."

I open the tube, smear some bright red lipstick onto my lips, and continue to smile at her.

47

"Oh, honey. You are too beautiful."

Meds then dispensed, she quickly pops them into her mouth and swallows. Then she tightens her hood around her face, stands up nodding her head, not taking her eyes off of my lips as she rises and leaves the room. And I realize in that moment I have never seen Linda's hair. For a sixty-five year old woman, she has a good-looking face, the wrinkles making her look wise. And those blue eyes that stick out in the world. But what about her hair? What does it look like?

Does she think she's beautiful, too?

Another month later and it's spring; the weather gets much warmer. With the sunshine heating up Minneapolis, Linda's brown hood is finally removed to reveal her incredibly short hair. Her head is almost shaved, really. Linda tells me she cuts it herself, every day. She is forever taking scissors to her short, gray hair.

"Oh, honey. Do you like my hair? I cut it today," she says to me.

Did she forget that she cut her hair yesterday? Most likely. It's apparent that she doesn't remember how she showed me her hair yesterday as here she is, showing it to me again. Smiling at her as I smiled at her yesterday, I say, "Yes. It looks wonderful, honey." And she smiles back, then takes her meds without a fuss. She returns to the courtyard to puff-pop at her flavored cigarettes.

With the warmth approaching, I have to start wearing t-shirts. I don't like to do this, as my arms are full of scars I put there with a razor a few years before. I have my own mental illness. The residents don't know this, as the staff is not allowed to reveal their mental health conditions to them. With the growing heat, I start to feel off in my body, worried about how my arms will inevitably be shown, worried that the residents will spot them and get into an awkward conversation with me about them, or worse, refuse to take their meds from a "crazy" person.

Plus, the scars make me feel ugly. My skin, marred. My self-esteem about my beauty diminishes with each white line revealed.

Last night, walking outside to throw the trash away, Linda, as always, called me over to smoke a cigarette with her. Crossing my bare arms over my chest to hide the scars, to try to forget that they exist, to try to feel better in my body, I stood next to her and smoked. Near the planter box in the courtyard next to Linda's small body that forever squats in her green chair, we looked at nothing in particular in the air.

Linda said nothing, so we smoked in silence. As I put my cigarette out and began to walk away, Linda ruptured the silence and called out to me.

"Oh, honey, you are too beautiful to sleep," she said in her raspy voice. I wasn't quite sure what this phrase meant, and I was still taken aback by it. How did she know this was what I needed to hear? How did she know that, in that exact moment, I needed someone to tell me I was beautiful? My skin tingled in the early evening air. Hairs perked.

Linda looked up at me with her wide eyes. "Too beautiful to sleep, honey."

That was yesterday. It's about to happen again, today. Standing away from her, smoking my own cigarette, Linda is silent again, not muttering to herself or speaking to God. I'm standing in my own silence, thinking more about this body I do not like. I've been pacing around depression about my weight lately, how I believe I'm too fat, how I berate myself each time I eat. It's driving me crazy.

Just as I'm about to finish my cigarette and go into my office in order to avoid free dinner in the cafeteria, Linda turns her head to me and breaks the silence in that graveled voice of hers I used to be scared of, but now find soothing. "Oh, honey, your body is perfect just the way it is."

A little chill runs through my body. What can she see? What other layer of perception does she have? Linda senses something about me, and I open my heart up to her, wondering what else she knows about me.

"Your body is perfect, honey." She nods her head at me. Not knowing what else to do, I laugh and say thank you.

But that chill at her perception of what I need is still running through my body. Linda turns her head away from me, her signal that she wants to stop talking. I finish my cigarette in silence with her, and go back inside to try to pass out a few meds to clients who need them before dinner. In my office, I think about what Linda said about my body. Somehow my skin feels more acceptable, now. Now, the desire to not eat tonight evaporates.

One of the residents doesn't come into my office to take her diabetes medication like she always does before dinner. This woman who needs this big, white pill at 4pm is usually right on time, heaving her large body through my office door before dinner. But she's not here, so I go down to eat dinner, feeling positive about feeding this body that feels too-big because of what Linda has said. Afterward, the cafeteria closes for the night; I hand out meds to the other residents, and then it's 6pm and the diabetic woman still has not shown up. I go looking for her and find her in her room, sleeping. She wakes up at my three light taps on her door. She comes out of her room and instantly begins hurling curses at me, yelling because now she has missed dinner and she's diabetic and what if she dies?

This woman has never yelled at me before. In fact, none of the residents have yelled at me. My body doesn't know how to respond to her screams. Because the residents are always kind to me, always take their meds with smiles and strike up a conversation about such-and-such. They tell me they love me. But now here's this woman yelling at me, her face reddening to a shade as dark as her auburn hair. Her anger surprises me, as she is usually the nicest one of the bunch, the one who talks gleefully about her family and is always willing to help round up residents for med time if they are missing, or change the towel rack in the bathroom.

After she yells that I'm *a stupid fucking incompetent bitch*, she storms off down the hall to go have a cigarette. Walking the other way down the hall to my office, I'm surprised to see Linda standing around the corner. Her eyes look into mine and tell me, without words, that she heard the hollering. Entering the office, I sit in my chair, getting Linda's meds ready with my hands shaking. I'm on the verge of crying, but I try not to. I don't want Linda to see painful emotions weep out of me.

She sits down across from me. "Oh, honey," she says, "your face is turning red. Are you okay?"

"Fine, just a little hot."

She sits staring at me with her milky eyes as my hands continue to shake. And then a tear rolls down my cheek.

Linda slowly gets up and closes the door.

"Oh, honey, don't worry. People can be mean, here. It's their mental illness, honey. But you're an angel. It's okay to cry, honey. Just let it out. It's okay when we need to cry. God is here for you."

I cry, then swipe away at my eyes. I cry. Handing Linda her meds, I continue to cry. She repeats her soft words, gives me permission to show my emotions even though my supervisor would say this is unprofessional. But with Linda's words, her insistence that *it's alright to cry*, I start to loosen up a bit, begin to exhale the breath that was coming out of me in short spurts. Linda doesn't hug me, doesn't hold my hand. What she does is take her meds— one tab and capsule at a time—and ask for a cigarette. Wiping my tear-wetted palms on my jeans, I get two cigarettes and hand them over to Linda. She stands up and opens the door. Before she goes out, she looks back over her shoulder and says, "Honey, it is okay to cry."

In that moment, I stop crying.

An old schizophrenic woman sits in the courtyard at my work. Skinny legs cross over themselves, her body hunches forward in the green, plastic chair. No one else sits in this chair. The other residents know it is her favorite spot, and they do not want to make her angry. She has an explosive temper. She screams into the night air about sins against God, about rape and whores and stealing. But she doesn't scream at me, because I know something. What I know is this: While she has a diagnosis, she's not insane. She's just an honest and eccentric woman trying to figure out what to do with herself, with her pain. Perhaps, at times, it's okay to scream.

Coupons

The young pregnant black woman living in this transitional residency isn't sure how to use coupons. She's cutting them out anyway. Jalacia is six months pregnant and learning how to save money for her baby, which is essential as she doesn't have a job right now. She used to strip, but the pregnancy put her job on hold. Her hair color also went on hiatus since she found out she was pregnant. What used to be weaves of electric blue in the back, hot pink on the sides, and peroxide blonde bangs that hung down past her purple eyes have turned into simple, soft, curly black braided extensions. This has something to do with growing up, I imagine. Motherhood. She's just twenty years old. Too young to be growing up. And yet she is already too old for innocence.

Her body tells me this.

I see it.

I know I might never again see the red leopard paw prints she has tattooed on her dark flesh, starting from her ass and stepping their way up around her ribcage, traversing her chest and peaking at her shoulder. But I'll know they are there, know how her past is imprinted on her body. And her future has already started to imprint itself onto her flesh—the skin that stretches to contain the growing part of her. A new her.

Six months ago Jalacia gave me a fashion show. She stopped by my office one night on her way to work to show me her newest outfit. Silver fabric flashed across her body as she paraded around the room, laughing. A calypso of a stringy thing. It was the night after she got her leopard prints, the tattoos that swagger on her skin, revealed by the barely-there outfit, the shiny spandex fabric taut over her breasts. This: a strip of sparkling silver down her abdomen, showing flesh below hips, mostly covering her crotch, then more strings strung. They flew upward around her bony hips, connecting the stretch of silver that traveled along her lower regions, front to back. In the past six months, the silver has been replaced by baggy, pale pink cotton shirts. Elastic waist jeans.

I'm assuming she got these calm-downed clothes from a friend, or perhaps a family member she is still in contact with—one who did not kick her out or leave her when she was just a child, or simply disappeared or moved on or any of the ways that could have led to her homelessness. Whatever her story may be, it brought her here, to this transitional residency for homeless youth. Here, I am a night-staff counselor. Here, I am in my office, door open, encouraging any of the thirty-six residents to come in and chat with me about their problems. Trauma, family, anxieties.

I listen.

The story of Jalacia's life is learning a new language while she lives it. New events that translate her body's tale from one definition of pride to another. The body-confidence she held while stripping now shows through mature, pale pink cotton that compliments her confidence in how she'll be a good mother. I hope others believe the same thing, believe in Jalacia, too. That she can do this, can make single motherhood work for her. But she worries. Rightfully so. She's poor and running out of money and has three more months to wait until the baby comes out.

Thus, coupons.

I tell her how they work, how if there's a barcode then she needs to cut the coupon out and give it to the cashier when she checks out. This will give her the discount. I tell her how the ones without barcodes are just advertisements for what's on sale at the store this week.

After she borrows the office scissors to cut out what she thinks she'll use and hands them back to me, handle-first, safely, motherly, her dark, swollen hands holding the metal legs of the closed blades, she goes up to her unit to grab the cut-out posters of Disney characters, of Bible characters she's been coloring lately. Tomorrow, she'll laminate the finished images with packaging tape. But for now, she continues to color within the cartoon outlines. Soothed by the motion and mental space the mindless task provides, Jalacia considers colored pencils to be quite calming. Tranquil. She colors now, having returned to my office, sitting at the table behind me. This is what she does to occupy her time while she's not working, while she readies herself for her soon-to-be baby girl. But before that happens, Jalacia will tape the posters on the same wall as her baby girl's crib. Or at least where the crib will be. She hasn't purchased one yet. She's waiting to find a coupon for it.

On Grief

Stage 1: Denial

Rows of pews lined up with each other, precise, measured, like an orchard, like trunks perfectly spaced and queued, limbs extending towards the sun, towards each other, elongating, trying to reach, connect, stretching to umbrella the brown-leafed forest floor. How limbs swayed from dusk's heavy sighs. There, inside that church, sitting in those paralleled pews, sighs did arrive. Human exhalations. And the echoes of laments, too. Heavy moans pursued the realized fact of a life lost. What could be done? People populated each pew and swayed, too. Prayed. Outbreath of grief in oscillating waves extending towards the casket, wanting to connect with the deceased one last time. Then inhale. Then exhale. Bring breath into the body so the soul can finally face the depth of this tragedy. The car crash. The nineteen-year-old woman who died too soon, leaving the other half of a bestfriend pair behind.

The deeply grieving sat in front of her, heads bobbing back and forth, rocking, swaying to the sounds of the eulogy. Sitting in the back pew, hands postulating prayer, the rest of her was paralyzed by the power of death, by its efficiency to quickly wipe away from the world whichever enlivened being it chose. Her view was of the dismayed family. The men with their white and pale blue collars, the women with their black dresses, the children squirming in uncomfortable outfits meant to express respect for the dead. The parents and grandparents and uncles and aunts and next-door neighbors and the old teachers from high school were all there to pray for youth gone missing. Drowning in the disbelief that the young could leave this world before them, could diminish before their aging eyes. How her visage had vanished. The impossibility of one last look. The gruesome car crash. Closed casket.

After the funeral, not knowing what else to do, everyone stood around the back of the church, hanging bodies limp with woe on the wood paneled walls. No one said much, could say much. Eyes glossed over, gazing past each other, silent as they choked on memories. Palms clasped, kept close to their chests, as if each memory would soon evaporate from their bodies. Float away. As if they would forget her once they shed their denial. She weighed heavily on their hearts. Her death, then, a reference point of time. The *from then on*. The *after*.

Still sitting in the back, alone in the lonely pew, she closed her eyes to the tears about to burst, mind about to admit the harsh reality of permanence. How *from then on* she would no longer know understanding. She squeezed her eyelids closer together, harder, wanting to protect herself from seeing the power of death. She didn't see when it started to snow, when the white began to collect on the hearse, *after*.

Stage Two: Anger

Her stomach. Heavy. Hot. Full with what she just gushed in there, quickly. Consumed. Swallowed. The intention to turn inward on herself. She didn't know how else to function. Proceed. The parts of a dead father she now performs. But first, the prop she found that kicked it all off, incited her to take action. A liter of an empty bottle. How it lounged, casually, on the floor of her father's car. Correction: her *deceased* father's car. A recent event. But about the bottle: She had been traversing the driveway in a slumberly walk from outside cigarette to inside coffee. That's when she saw it. That's when she paused.

A whole-body pause.

An unrelenting pause.

A body stopped in motion when eyes that were aimlessly weaving around the sights of her surroundings happened to travel through the passenger side window of the widowed car.

Red label. Foreign. Russian. Exported vodka. Also, foreign as in never seen before.

An empty liter of obscure liquor led her to wonder how long her father had been hiding his imbibing.

She took in the details of the bottle's visage, memorized its shape, its curves. And the certain hue of red of the Russian label. Staring down at it through the glass, she didn't see anything special about this bottle of vodka, other than how it was his preference. And now it would be hers.

Soon, shortly after she returned from the nearest liquor store, she would chug and gulp and both things would singe memories of him in her life. She would be drunk with liquor and anger, which would quickly transform her sight red, swiftly bloodshot the whites of her eyes, like his always were. She would remember that detail. His glaring eyes that lasered into hers on that one day when she stared down the truth of his relapse. His decades-long relapse.

She downed a liter of a full bottle.

Then, she felt a connection with her father. Then, she put his liquor, his disease, those memories, all inside of her until she could feel something about him residing within her. How she pushed the alive version of him away. How she wanted to pull him back in, stow him within her body so also she could finally feel what it meant to deeply love someone. She got her own bottle, drank her own bottle on her own. Drank to feel how he must have felt when he drank himself to death. Blood alcohol level: 0.46. With each glug, her throat burned, her insides ripped. Scream. And it felt good. Still feels good. That jagged tear that felt something like him, then her.

Stage Three: Depression

It is the morning of the funeral. The sky threatens to rip open when nothing inside of her can. Hardened, her emotions froze when he decided to give up, to let go, to tend to his suicidal tendencies. After many failed previous attempts, life let him win. It gave up. She always thought this would happen, his dying. Suicide.

It is the morning of his funeral, and she's wearing a black shirt with a black skirt and black flats too tight on her feet. Her skin suffers. She suffers. She thinks this is what one is supposed to do for a funeral. Wear black. Suffer. Or, at least show something that looks like suffering. The black confirms this. She knows she's supposed to be mourning right now. But that sounds tiring and time-consuming. She can't find the want within her to do this. Yet, she goes. Yet, she "grieves." Puts on the mourning show. Pleases those—the ones she mocks—as she places sad expressions on her face.

Earlier on in the morning of her father's funeral, she had to dig around for that black skirt. She wasn't even sure she owned it anymore, wasn't quite sure what she was doing in the tangle of boxes and clothes and belts torn down from the top shelf of her childhood closet. She remembered it, though, the skirt. It was the one she wore to her interview for college. The skirt in which she hoped to look serious. Like she meant it. Like she wanted that acceptance. And now like she wanted to go to his funeral. After a collection of minutes spent searching, she finally found the skirt tucked beneath a small stack of clothes kept stowed away for grownup events. Job interviews. Weddings. Deaths. The clothes of a woman. Costumes. She put the skirt on. Slipped into the other black accoutrements to play the part of a grieving daughter. She stepped outside. Looked up. The sky was growling, threatening to relinquish a welled-up wetness.

Now, at her father's funeral, she sits in a pew, not feeling any wetness that could—or perhaps should—well up inside her. She doesn't have to wonder why this is. It's simply the fact of him. Because he was the father who she recognized as such. He was, after all, never there for her. She sits, rock heavy, her hands placed in the lap of her black skirt. She waits in the pews with people who weep, people who want to be there. The preacher is about to arrive. A preacher who was hired just for this occasion, to say memorable things about a man he never met, about a man she wished she could forget. She sits, cemented. She looks around at the small crowd composed of people she has never met. Golf partners, business partners, people who were partners with him during his momentary bout of sobriety, until he decided to give up on that, too, to turn away from those who wanted to help. She thinks of this, of how he turned away, how he twisted away from her, from the family, from anything labeled *Life*. Her stomach turns at this. Sours.

She realizes something. How he'll never again turn away, and how his body was turned and twisted in its final, gray position. This thought twists inside of her. Pinches. Her hardened exterior, the cement wall she built between her body and this world begins to crumble. Fall. An actress playing the part of angry daughter, using conjured disgust to protect the places inside of her that she now knows will miss him. How, at one point, she reveled in calling him *daddy*. Now gone. But it's been gone for a while. Been gone so long that she barely re-members what it was that, at one point, she loved about him. But now he's gone. Reparations cannot be made. A seriousness swells inside of her, a feeling that is rightfully dressed in black. Anger that once seethed now smolders. Something melts inside of her. He is gone. This weighs heavily on her shoulders. Her whole body. And that is when she feels it. Her eyes. Her staring-off, motionless eyes that are now trying to avoid what she knows is about to happen. It growls inside of her. Threatens. She opens up to the idea of opening up. Of grieving. She lets the sky break inside of her. She lets it rain.

Stage Four: Resignation

He is a stubborn old man. He still has all of his faculties. He winks. He is lying there on the hospital bed, lying there to be taken care of. He is waiting for his time, a line she hates to hear. His time is near. Her grandfather is old enough to naturally say a final goodbye. It's been ninety years since he first opened his eyes. The past twenty-eight were spent watching her when he could, when her family visited him. His eyes on her the little grandbaby girl body, the freckles spreading themselves out across the years. She saw his features slowly grow. Wrinkles rising like a shifting earth, mountains creating valleys wet with rain, soft with the moist eyes of the elderly. She is there to take care of him because her mother can't be here. She needs a break from her dying father.

Here, she takes care of her mother's father in what-ever way she can. Adjusts his mask. The face he tries to free. He wants to breathe, normally. He wants to speak.

She listens to his garble, his desires fallen numb on his motionless tongue. She watches his body rise and fall with machines, and she sees the body as its own machine. Outdated, needing repairs, the soft wear and tear on his mind. She looks down on his body, concaved, and her eyes swell, little lakes tucked in her own valleys of slowly growing skin.

He motions for a pen. She gives it to him, places a small pad of paper in his lap so he can tell her something. Perhaps, hopefully, he'll tell her what happened during those seventeen hours he was alone, stuck on the floor. After the stroke hit him, internal electricity ricocheted through his spine. He was alone, on the floor, the phone ringing down the hall. Seventeen hours. Now he does not, cannot write. His right arm, like his eyes, like his tongue, has lost its touch. The right side of his body has permanently paused. Paralyzed. She touches his left hand, encourages the pen to hit page. Instead, he mumbles, tears off the mask and says something like coffee. He winks with his one good eye. She accepts the wink as a knowing. She lets go of his arm, lets go of the connection she knows is about to go. Vanish. She takes the pen. She puts it down.

Stage Five: Acceptance

It is morning. It's time to rise differently. Meet morning with open eyes instead of the heavy lids of late. A refreshing, promising morning breath in a time when the fact of breathing has tormented her, has kept going even when she feels like death. As where night swallows day. But recently she's looked forward to how morning will blast night away.

It is morning. It's time to rise differently. She swings her legs out of bed, meets the body of her dog, the animal's susurrus snoring. Half-awake breath. The dog wakes up when she lightly unfurls her toes on the pet's stomach. A head rises. Shifting further off the bed, she gazes back with eyes that finally want to open. She yawns herself awake. The old dog yawns along. Old as in 12, as in 84, if the dog is counting. The animal's days are drawing to a close, but neither being knows when. Perhaps old dog eyes will open and close for many years more. Or perhaps for just another day.

It is morning. She places her feet away from the dog's body, gives her legs room to stand. The dog rolls over, a tummy expecting to be rubbed. Hips shift, joints creak and grind with memories of youthful leaps and sprints. She bends down, rubs the outstretched belly with a smile she can't resist as each day helps her to roll away from recent moments of mourning.

It is morning. It's time to rise differently. She clomps across the room, hips waking and adjusting to holding her weight instead of weighing down the bed. She raises her fists to her eyes, rubs away the morning crusties, feels for the luggage underneath her eyes. Frog eyes. There is nothing there for her to feel. Eyes no longer go to sleep depleted of energy, exhausted from nights spent dreading morning. Another day rolls along. She has learned how to roll with it. Her index finger swipes away those remainders of sleep, those dried specks of dissipating tears. Disappearing tears. They continue to fade. Sadness slowly lifts from her, day-by-day.

It's morning. She rises differently. It's a morning in which she continues to move away from mourning. To move into a body that knows it's alive.

Howls

"You know, Chels. I would walk through a ball of *fire* for you."

Six years later I will use this phrase when I write his obituary.

"A ball of *fire*, Chels. A ball of *fire*." I am fifteen when my father sits slouched in his bed, when he slurs these words to me, fumes of vodka spewing from his tongue. He sloshes the phrase, my name towards my stonewalled face as if the repetition might make me feel different. As if I wouldn't despise him despite the fact that he is a father who terrorizes my skin. A man who sits in his bed all day, drunk, screaming about his need to disappear. The suicide he craves. How his words, his painful wails, mean nothing to me. As I look at him, the mess of his body and the meaningless words his intoxication exhibits to me, I sense his need to recede. Retreat from life. Yes, please that. After he establishes the ball of fire I know he would never walk through, I spit at him what it is I want him to do.

My grandfather speaks to me for the first time in two hours. "Have a good time, Chelsey." I climb out of his truck and open the door to his secluded mountain cabin. I will be here for a week, alone. I am here to rest, to breathe, to relax, to soak in the serenity of the jagged horizon. An endless mountain range. To regain a desire to live. After my grandfather waves his hand out the window, he drives the two hours back to the city. Aside from the good time he wished me, there were no other words we shared.

What could he possibly say to his suicidal, nineteen-year-old granddaughter?

He leaves.

I am alone.

I look out at the mountains.

I think about falling into them, their silence.

I think about my father.

I think about dying.

I drink vodka.

I do not have a good time.

Because now it is later on that night and my head is in my arms, my arms are smashed into the blue plaid couch, my dead-feeling knees dig into the living room floor. And my chest heaves in and out. In and out. See-sawing. My lungs grasping for air. The gulping inflations, the rasping deflations. I choke on the couch cushions. I am wailing. This is about my father. This is about how he keeps threatening suicide. This is about how I wish he would do it already. And while my screams echo throughout this empty cabin, my own suicidal urges overpower them, create a cacophony of gruesome images.

I am nineteen and the sounds of a constantly drunk and suicidal father rattle in my ears. Even in this silence they send me crashing to the floor.

I wail.

I drink more vodka.

I wail some more.

And then I wake up in the morning to find my body slouched on the couch. This idea of being alone for a week to recover from a suicide attempt did not work. I grab the phone.

"Grandpa, will you come pick me up?" My voice cracks as I try not to cry.

"Oh. Well. Yup. I'll leave right now." His scratchy reply.

It is two hours later. He picks me up. There are no questions, no judgments. Just another silence filling his truck.

Those two hours of silence roll by easily. We arrive at his house in the city. The idea of a hug hangs in the air, but we say nothing to each other.

It is that 3am hour between night and day. Lightless. I am twenty-seven. My father has been dead for six years. It is five degrees below zero outside. In my apartment, I shoot up from bed, alerted by a collection of disturbing sounds. My dog is howling at my neighbor, who is also howling. I shush my dog so I can hear what all is going on. Aside from the neighbor's howling, there are also stern voices. They rumble right next to my door, the deep sounds stationed in the hallway. My dog quiets as I silently slink to the front room, not wanting to make a noise. I do not want my disturbed neighbor and the source of the deep voices to know I am here, on the other side of the door, listening. Silently. I don't want to give away my position. I want to stay hidden. Undisturbed. To avoid interacting with this howling woman. I cannot

handle her screams. I have been through enough screaming, a lifetime of listening to guttural expressions of pain.
They terrify me. When I listen to her wails, when the panic
rises in me from knowing these sounds so deeply, when
the flashbacks of my father arrive, when I can sense my
plead for please, not again, not these sounds, I quickly
need something to quell my frightened body.

I light up a cigarette. Because I can. I creep up to my
peephole to take in the scene. Two uniformed men standing. One disheveled woman slouching. She is still howling.
The cops are not howling. They stand with their hands on
their hips, or rather their holsters. They look down at this
shattering woman and try to ask questions between each
roar, to get an answer for Why? She pays no attention,
sucks in more breath and continues her screams. They
speak down to her. *Ma'am. Where do you live?* They are
stern, yet curious. No, not curious. Confused, mostly, by
this woman howling in the hallway. I, too, am confused.
And at 3am, my dog stands next to me, ears perked, tail
still alert, steadily staring at the door. I briefly look down
at her. She pays no attention to me, is too distracted by
the din. I smoke my cigarette and listen to the sound of
one woman's body breaking down.

The cluster headaches attack the entire maze of my
father's nerves. They start from the neck and lead to his
temples. Pain creeps behind his eyes, pulsates. Stays for
hours. Days. The desire to live breaks down. A squeeze, a
tug, a yanking on every nerve. The pain is too much. He
wants to die. He waits for this to occur. Though perhaps

he will do something about this soon. It is getting to that point. Until then, he stays in his chambers, his room all day long, drinking liquor and praying it will assuage his screeching brain. Thirteen years of sobriety surrendered to self-medicate his pain.

But the vodka always wears off.

So he does something else, takes a different approach to relieve his anguish.

He screams.

A howling crashes through our walls. Guttural growls. Waves of deafening wails.

His shrieks ricochet through the house, reverberate down my spine. I shake with each shriek. Another roar. My body quivers as he screams through the pain.

My grandfather has moved his lips much in his life. They cannot hold back the lyrics. Lips partially open, lips surrounded by silence soon to be no more. Lips lined with the creases of octogenarian skin. Now, they rest motionless in the stage front of his face, knowing their cue is coming up.

They cannot resist the song.

Before the FBI, before law school, before my mother, before his marriage, before the Navy, my grandfather stood in church, singing. A young man finding his voice.

He finds it now.

The melody comes slipping out, a mist at first, the lyrics mumbled. But only momentarily. The TV across the room from him sits silent, staring at him, giving him the stage.

The opening of the throat. Esophagus, lungs, tongue, teeth, and those old man lips all move, the motion ignited by his memories. His baritone voice bursts through his house, a deep vibration bringing him back to those times when he was just a young man singing in a choir, testing how his voice inhabited the world.

My mother, grandmother and I stop our chatter at the kitchen table to listen to his spiritual song spill out of the living room. Our faces transition from relaxed smiles to stunned expressions. Awe.

And then it is over. He returns to the muted TV, silently watching.

We all have our sounds. One neighbor snores through my walls, another has sex through my ceiling. I do not know what people can hear of me.

In my apartment building, we keep to ourselves most of the time. A nod in the hallway, perhaps. Sometimes a comment about the weather, the foliage, the construction on our street, the raised rent, the *etcetera*. Nameless neighbors, remote residents, our lives silently slipping past each other as we traverse the hallway to our own apartments, our places where we feel protected. At home.

And then this. A woman screaming. A woman making the presence of her pain, her refusing-to-be-silent body well known. At 3am she claims the hallway as the place to announce her pronounced misery, the wretchedness over something raging inside of her. Her anguish too agonizing to keep quiet about. She breaks down the protective borders of a should-be pleasant building. I do not know what my neighbors are doing in this moment, if they, too, shot up from bed and are now standing in the middle-of-the-night darkness in their own apartments, concealed by turned-off lamps, trying to get a glimpse of her screeching body through their own peepholes. One eye shut, one eye straining to see. An eerie stillness. I cannot hear their motions, the sounds of their movements silenced by her screams. But I can feel their presence pulsating around me, their shocked and alert bodies pressing against their doors. We surround her. We silently gawk at her screams in the supposed safety of our own homes, hidden behind our front doors. But the wood does not shield us from her howls. We stand alone, separated by flimsy drywall, collectively listening, anxiously breathing, too stunned to know what else to do with this destroyed woman, this nameless neighbor breaking.

My father's eyes never talk to me.

They do not glance my way. I am an image he always avoids. Later on in my life, six years after his death, my mother will say this to me: *He never wanted children.* Her admission will tentatively approach me as she carefully places those words into the air, the words that will become the proof of why his eyes refused to notice me. The evidence will be shown, the information known, the explanation delayed by just a couple of decades.

But it is before I know this when I recognize how his eyes always avoid mine. It is six years before his ~~suicide~~ death (suicide?—how else to define death by alcohol poisoning?) that my role of daughter is forever slipping away from his life. And "father" is not a part he plays either. He has no desire to take on that role. He does not ask about school, my softball games, or my relationships. He does not know my best friend's name. We have been friends for three years, and she didn't even know I had a father. She has never seen him.

And he never looks at me.

I am not there to see my grandfather fall. I am not there to answer my grandmother's phone call. I am not there to help him off the floor. In fact, I am not there to see him at all.

There he is, on the floor.

Seventeen hours he lies on the floor, his ninety-year-old body collapsed into the scratchy blue carpet. The phone rings down the hall.

Seventeen hours after the stroke hits him he remains motionless in the mountain cabin, alone, perhaps hoping someone will come help him.

Seventeen hours slip by; seventeen hours march past the time he said he would return. My grandmother starts to worry. Yesterday, my grandfather left for his mountain cabin, insisting on fixing the small holes in the roof, alone. She is not aware of the stroke, yet fears its occurrence. She calls the closest neighbor, the one with the red A-frame house. He lives ten miles away by car, two miles as the crow flies. She calls him to check in on the old man.

Seventeen hours after the fact, he is still alone.

In my mind, I am there. In my mind, I stand there frozen, watching from down the hall, letting the phone ring. I stand there staring at him, not knowing how to help, taking in a full view of his pain, gazing at the carpet he is crumpled on, the scratchy blue fabric my own knees burrowed into when I was alone in this cabin six years ago, wailing. In my mind, I am witness to this moment in which my grandfather begins to die. I see myself standing there, stock-still, trying to grasp the slowly unfurling meaning of his life now leaving.

This is what I am told: The neighbor arrives twenty minutes after my grandmother's call. He sees my grandfather on the floor, lifts the stricken body, carries it to his truck. For now, my grandfather is still alive. There is a race to the nearest town's hospital, then a swift helicopter ride to the hospital in the city, the one with a better intensive care unit, the one in which, three weeks later, my grandfather will die in room 609. I will be there for that. For that, I will stand, stare, look, stay frozen in my helplessness. His paralyzed tongue, his motionless face and lips. His voice that becomes a deep rumbling, a barely-audible mumbling.

And there will be no more singing, no movement from his throat. Esophagus, lungs, tongue, teeth, and those old man lips will all close. Collapse.

In this silence, though, I hear his spirit speak. It wants to go home.

What it is I hear: his body crashing down. The demolition of a house. There is the cemented tongue, the power-outaged brain, the disintegrating insulation, the frame of the visible ribs that crack under the weight of age. The floorboards of his elderly bones groan. He can no longer ignore the severity of this withering home. The screams of cellular breakdown. The sound of a body breaking. This, I hear.

I continue to watch my neighbor howling through my peephole. Her body trembles, her flesh unable to contain whatever pain. A story held within her body must have gone wrong. A miserable ending she could do nothing about. And so she drank. Now she screams.

I smoke my cigarette because I do not know what else to do.

I do not want to disturb her.

Creep.

I am fifteen when my mother orders me to go talk to my father because he is threatening suicide, again. She is sick of dealing with it, sick of hearing about his misery. I take my anger into his room. I surge through his bedroom door and find my father in bed, slouched against a pile of pillows that protect his back from the bars of the brass bed frame. His eyes are steady on the TV, as if he is in serious conversation with it, as if he is trying to make a point. The salesperson inside of him incapable of letting go of the habitual eye contact he makes with things important to him.

But the rest of him looks a little lost, a little like he landed in this room unsure of what, exactly, it is he is supposed to do here. His legs are tangled in the sheets on his bed, his arms flop to his sides. The TV blares in a chilling silence across the room, a golf tournament.

My dying grandfather needs to pee. I stand above him bearing witness to this desperation. He claws at the plastic white Depends with his barely functioning left hand, thinking they are his underwear that need removing. He rips and wrangles the diaper off.

He yanks out his old man penis and holds it. The stream of brown urine sputters across his skeletal thigh barely the size of my arm. I do nothing. I stand and watch. I hover over him bearing witness to the muddy, liquid proof of his cells breaking down. We do not give him food or water. His tongue is too paralyzed to swallow. Liquid kept out of his body for two weeks now.

He sighs. Surrenders.

I ran into my neighbor a couple of times outside of our building as we walked our dogs. Her dog's name is Ce-Ce. I do not remember my neighbor's name. And I do not hear Ce-Ce barking right now, making noise about the noise her owner makes. I would think a loyal dog would make its voice heard as it responded to its owner's outcry. But, unlike my own moaning dog, Ce-Ce is silent. A thought: Perhaps she's dead. Perhaps the dog's absence is what spurred my neighbor's lament. Perhaps.

My neighbor looks like she's either fifty or sixty or seventy years old. I cannot tell. As I stare at her through my peephole, my hands braced against my door, smoke from my cigarette curling into my eye, I cannot make out

Chelsey Clammer

her age. Her hair has some gray. An army of wrinkles dominates her face. There is her coarse voice, perhaps acquired from a lifetime spent smoking. Her bulbous nose is red, blood vessels bursting.

She has the nose of an alcoholic.

Peeping through my peephole, taking in this scene through a sliver of fish-eyed glass, I briefly wonder if I should help the officers, if I should inform them that she lives behind that door she is slouched against. They look down at her, hands still on their holsters, not quite knowing what to do with this woeful woman.

I say nothing. I do nothing. I remain in my apartment, smoke my cigarette.

I shout my father's name towards the lump of his body lying in bed, the body that houses the history of his cluster headaches, alcoholism, bipolar disorder. I ask what it is he thinks he's doing, why it is he's so drunk, again.

"Chels." My father's eyes sweep over the white walls, his wooden dresser, me. They are unable to focus on anything. His head slinks to his right shoulder, swings along the trajectory of his rounded chin, and jerks back up to its starting position. "I just don't want to live." There is an accumulation of spittle at the corners of his mouth.

"Yeah, whatever," I hiss.

I'm fifteen and sick of my father threatening suicide.

And then I say it.

"Kill yourself already."

He continues to sit in bed.

But then he makes a slight turn of his neck.

He looks at me.

Six years after my father ~~killed himself~~ died from alcohol toxicity, I stand in room 609.

My grandfather continues to crumble. The legs go first. Knees begin to look more like elbows. The door begins to close in his mind. His eyes, the window panes, fog over, become milky and clouded. The water leaks. The plumbing, uncontrollable.

I continue to stand in room 609.

I'm sure I make noises my neighbors also do not want to disturb. The occasional heaves as I hold onto bulimia one last time. *Law & Order* blares. The vibrator as it whirls. The sobs over a father. The grief over a silenced grandfather, exponentiated. The silence is bloated with an unavoidable mourning. Grief. But I do not growl at the memories. I have seen how howling doesn't help, is hopeless. Instead, I distract myself with the remaining hurls from a lingering eating disorder, with the staged sirens from the television show that blare inside my bedroom, with the buzzing vibrations trying to stimulate my flesh. These are the sounds I exude, the tones that penetrate the thin protection of my walls, my home. I consider these noises to be considerate. I could be disturbing my neighbors, could be breaking the sound barrier with my roaring desperation. I do not do that. Though sometimes slight yips slip out. I cannot fully contain the pains of grief. Cannot fully muffle this agonizing, unsteady growl.

The man continues to look at me.

And then he says, "I would walk through a ball of fire for you, Chels. A ball of *fire*."

The repetition means nothing to me.

After I demand that my father die, after he makes repetitive and drunken declarations about a ball of fire, I stomp away and slam the bedroom door behind me, expecting—no, *praying*—to hear a gunshot accompany the sound.

There is silence.

I hesitate outside his door, hovering, listening for some sound I think might be there.

I hear nothing.

I detect the stillness emanating from his bedroom. Sense his heart still beating. But his body and mind are slowly disintegrating, crumbling. They do so silently, subtly. The old mattress creaks, wears away.

As the minutes slip by after the slammed door, I begin to feel let down. He probably returned his gaze to the TV, forgetting what just happened. Maybe my presence didn't even register in his mind. Maybe he never really saw me. Maybe now he simply remains a drunk man slouched in bed, watching a silent TV.

His body is barely moving.

And I am leaving. It is time for me to return to my home. I cannot stay with my grandfather any longer. It has been three weeks since the fall. I must go.

He lies in his hospital bed before me as he has been lying in this hospital for three weeks now. His eyes are closed. I lean down to kiss his forehead. As my lips touch his wrinkles, his eyes jolt open. I take a step back. He looks up at me for a second, the soft blue irises diving into mine. Then, he reaches out with his barely-working left arm and grabs me in for a powerful hug. He has never hugged me in this way before, has never ensconced my body with this much strength. With his hand tight around my waist, he holds me close to his body. Then, somehow, miraculously his paralyzed tongue momentarily thaws. He says something to me. A whisper enters my ear.

I love you.

I pull back with goose-bumped flesh. This, he has never said to me. He releases his arm from around my waist. It flops to his side. I take a step back. Our eyes stare into each other again. One set of eyes is almost dead, the other cannot control this oncoming wet.

I walk out of room 609, unknowingly carry my body to the parking lot. Autopilot. I am distracted by one thought: I will never see him again. The automatic doors open, the hot air hits my face, and this is when the tears finally arrive, spill. The sun strikes my skin, warming the wet streaks of my grief.

Cigarette ash hisses in the cup of water I use as an ashtray. The sound startles me, speaks to something swirling inside me. Because I have been holding back my own howling lately, holding back the pain of what it was like to hear my father shriek and groan, to watch the life of my grandfather drain out of his body. But holding the howls inside makes the pain grow louder.

It has been a half hour now and the woman continues to cry. But the sound has diminished a bit. Her wails have turned into small puffs of whimpers. The police officers left, perhaps bored by her refusing-to-be-moved body. The clamor coming from this woman eventually ends. She is still slouched in front of her door, but the struggle diminishes. Her lips relax. Now she is sleeping. Passed out. I extract myself from my peephole view, but immediately shut my eyes against the image of witnessing her agony. The din is in me. I do not want to let it out, do not want to disturb my neighbors tonight. We have heard enough. I creep around my apartment, my body pacing along the carpet.

Creep.

I do not want to disturb.

Do not want to be like my father.

So I do my howling quietly, hoping that by holding it in the world will be appeased. Will not force others to hear my pain. I know that sound, know how it wants to ooze from my body. But I also know how the howling doesn't help, how its release does nothing but terrorize flesh. So no, do not disturb. Do not loudly leak.

And so I creep.

Restricted

- He was always saying "tomorrow."
- "I'll start my diet tomorrow."
- Mom: "Why not now?"
- Dad: "Tomorrow."
- Cookies, donuts, three servings of spaghetti. He would start the Cabbage Soup Diet tomorrow.
- Cluster headaches are worse than migraines; they squeeze every nerve from neck to temple and last for hours, sometimes days.
- He will die with scabs on his forehead from trying to rub away the pain.
- My dad drank to ease the cluster headaches.
- My dad was an alcoholic.
- Alcohol and pain made him take his life away.
- Mom: "When are you going to stop drinking?"
- Dad: "Tomorrow."
- He tried to be good for a week. No sweets. No liquor. He caved. He binged. He suffered.
- What tomorrow was supposed to bring:
- Lose weight fast!
- Low-fat and high-fiber for quick weight loss!
- Get slim now!
  - Day One: Fruits (no bananas), cabbage soup

- Day Two: Vegetables, soup, *and the reward of a baked potato with butter!*
- Day Three: Fruit, veggies, and soup
- Day Four: Bananas, skim milk, soup
- Day Five: Beef, tomatoes, soup
- Day Six: Beef, veggies, soup
- Day Seven: Brown rice, unsweetened juices, soup
- *Then stuff, stuff, stuff yourself!*
- Tomorrow.

Seven days after the tomorrow finally began and he would *stuff stuff stuff!* He did not stop stuffing until my mother nagged him about his eating habits, again. Once a month they had the tomorrow argument.

Alcohol and food. His vices. Intense suffering (detox) to try to alleviate the pain (head). Intense restriction (diet) to try to suspend the inevitable decline (body).

My father died of alcohol poisoning. He had been sober for a week, being good and clean, then his body snapped back into the binging routine. His autopsy report stated he was overweight.

Perhaps the alcohol contributed to weighing him down.

Question, Part 1: How much liquor can a 250-pound man drink before the toxicity kills him?

Answer, Part 1: About 30 drinks.

Question, Part 2: How much vodka did a 250-pound man drink in one night in order to end up—and literally *to end*—with a 0.46 blood-alcohol level?

Answer, Part 2: Do you really want to know?

- Suffer.
- Binge.
- Wash. Rinse. Repeat.
- Sober for a week. Fit for a week. Then.
- Restriction increases anxiety. Anxiety prompts binging.
- Binging is the dark side of restriction.
- This was the dark side of his life, the side that always showed itself, that shined the brightest.

The Zone Diet

Her thighs are suctioned into her navy blue spandex shorts. Her floral thong leotard clings to her body; her sweat clings to the fabric.

My mother bounces on the stage in front of me and the twenty other students in her Jazzercise class. We are in the basement of a church. It is a Wednesday night. She brings me to her class after she picks me up from school. Because I am a teenager with some babysitting experience, I come to her classes to watch the mothers' children for an hour while they desperately try to sweat back into their pre-children bodies.

Tonight there are no children, and so I join my mother for the hour-long class.

My mother immediately hits her Jazzercise groove, that concentrated and expert zone in which her body moves with precision and ease. She tackles each routine with enthusiasm and skill and still has enough breath to call out the instructions. She practices these routines forty hours a week. She is in shape. She is in her zone.

The Zone Diet:
- "Lose fat and increase wellness by reducing cellular inflammation."
- Get out of the "fat trap."
- Meal plan:
  1. 1/3 of the plate should consist of low-fat protein.
  2. 2/3 of the plate should consist of carbohydrates (fruits and vegetables).
- "The Zone recipes tempt your taste buds and satisfy hunger for four plus hours."

When we get home from her Jazzercise class, my mother finds my father eating a whole bag of chocolate chip cookies in their bed. He has broken his week-long diet, again. Tonight, we aren't able to tell whether he is drunk or not. Not yet. The sugar conceals his breath. She berates him about his diet. I go upstairs to my room, not wanting to listen to this argument again. As I get to my door, I hear her usual words: *No ice cream. No cookies. No donuts. If you're hungry, eat an apple.*

There are always bowls of fresh fruit and jars of nuts on our kitchen counter. Healthy snacks. It's what her *Zone* book tells her to do. Protein and carbohydrates, she wants to keep her body running at its peak performance. She needs all the energy she can get to put up with him. She tries to set an example for my father. Don't drink. No sweets. Exercise.

Once a month he will follow this plan for almost a week. And then he will not. And all the while my mother is in her zone, her anger at him grows as her fat cells recede. A growling stomach. More room in her body for anger, for her emotions to growl.

Ten years of this fight.

He dies. And the fight ends. And I am not sure who won.

After my father dies of alcohol poisoning, we find desserts hidden throughout the house. We excavate the house, spend two days filling a trash bag with stale cookies and empty liquor bottles.

The first night after my father died, I went into the kitchen and found his ice cream in the freezer. I devoured the whole carton standing in front of the refrigerator, wanting to feel something in my body, anything but the numb, the grief. I engulfed the ice cream, and instantly got a brain freeze. There, something. After this food binge, I drank vodka until I passed out. The next morning I began to restrict, to make my body show how it was that I felt. Empty. Hollow. Gone.

"The Marya Hornbacher Diet"

"The anoretic operates under the astounding illusion that she can escape the flesh, and, by association, the realm of emotions." –Marya Hornbacher, *Wasted*

Breakfast:

- 1 grapefruit (100 calories)

Lunch:

- 2 fat-free pretzels from a bag (20 calories)
- 4 carrot sticks (12 calories)
- 4 celery sticks (5 calories)
- 3 tsp of mustard (5 calories)
    - Total: 42 calories

Dinner:

- ½ cup of fat-free, sugar-free yogurt (60 calories)
    - Total: 60 calories

Total: 202 calories, 0 grams of fat

Restriction increases anxiety; anxiety prompts binging.
I have tried this diet. It turned me into a bulimic.
Wash. Rinse. Repeat. The cycle spirals.

Side note: A pro-ana (as in, yeah to anorexia) organization created this diet, named it after the author who gave anorexia a voice. They need to rename it. I lived with Marya. She did not eat like this. She lived like how I wanted to live—in the world, and with a body.

The Master Cleanse

- One day changed my life. It was that one day of a father found dead. Twenty-one years of knowing him, and our relationship suddenly changed within one day.
- One day.
- Despised when he was alive. Confused when he died. A 180 of a relationship. Six feet under.
- At what point do the memories of a drunk father fully leave your flesh? When will the toxic memories be cleansed?

It has been three years since my father's death. I have been trying the "Marya Hornbacher Diet" for three years. It is not going well. It is just before I experience the dark side of restriction (the binging, the purging, the wash, rinse, repeat) and I attempt the Master Cleanse. I feel something building up inside of me. I want it out.

For months, years after my father dies, I am in the zone of self-destruction. Odious amounts of alcohol. Blackened lungs. A stomach eating itself away. After my father dies, this is my zone, the only way I know how to live. My cells bloat with alcohol. I run off the hangovers. I have my pack-a-day. I have my drinks at night. My mouth consumes 1/3 nicotine and 2/3 liquor. Every day. Wash. Rinse. Repeat. Get it out of me. Get him out of me.

- This is not an emotional diet.
- Ingredients for the Master Cleanse:

1. Fresh squeezed lemon juice
2. Rich maple syrup
3. Cayenne pepper
4. Water
5. Laxatives
6. Salt

- I am twenty-four and in my room the day before I have promised myself I will start the Master Cleanse. Tomorrow, I will be good. Tomorrow I will start.

I sit on my window sill, window open, exhaling nicotine from my mouth in between gulps of vodka. I do not want to give these things up. The drunk. The numb. The intoxication. That muted grief within me. Or maybe I do want to give them up, but not permanently. Maybe for just a week, for just enough time to remember what it felt like when I was not stuffing myself with liquor.

- Tomorrow.
- The next day I start the Master Cleanse while hung over. The salt water flush pushes brown liquid out of my intestines for hours, days.
- Something is weeping out of me. I am too fatigued to figure out what it is.
- I sleep a ton. No dreams of my father. Perhaps the cleanse is working.
- I feel dazed, zoned out.

- My tongue turns white from the toxins being released through it. The taste of my father's death slowly seeps out of me.
- Day Four: I tell my therapist (the one I see once a week who specializes in eating disorders, not the one I see three times a week who specializes in grief and trauma) how great I feel on the Master Cleanse.
- "That diet will kill you. Especially with an active eating disorder. Your electrolytes will get off balance. You will die."
- I stop the cleanse right then.
- I am quickly out of my restriction zone.
- Straight from therapy I go to a bar.
- I am back in the zone I know so well.
- This zone does not and will not restrict the pain. Though what I hope for it to do is to extract this agony from my flesh.
- To cleanse myself of the grief.
- To deal with the grief instead of drinking it away.
- That is my goal.
- I will start it soon.
- Tomorrow.

Vaginatarian

She doesn't know if eating this is okay.

She suspects she might be breaking the rules.

She is a vegetarian.

No living things inside her mouth.

However, she is going down on a woman for the first time, wondering if she would still be able to call herself a vegetarian were she to eat a part of this living thing that is lying in front of her face. Could one be a cunt chomper *and* a vegetarian?

A moral dilemma.

Two years ago, at the age of fifteen, she decided to become a vegetarian because of that one image she got in her head that one night while she was eating that one hamburger: biting a cow's ass. As in: tearing a good chunk of rump flesh away with her teeth.

And the cow's ass bled.

And the raw hide was chewy.

And this is what we call a visceral image.

This visceral image of gnawing on animal flesh is what disgusted her. But, it is not what made her a vegetarian. No, it was something else. That something else was another particular image that quickly segued from the eating of the cow's ass scene: biting off a piece of human flesh.

Her father's forearm, specifically.

Yick.

There was no eating of the meat from that point on.

It is two years later. She is still a vegetarian. She is still not putting once-alive things near her mouth. But what is coming near her mouth now, at this point in time, is not a once-alive thing, but a currently *alive* thing, and she wonders how this fact might change the rules. She's on her stomach, on her bed, looking head-on at a crotch that is becoming increasingly less patient as each eyelash-length of a second blinks by and she's still lying there, motionless, not knowing if she can morally dive in.

Pros:
- consummate relationship with girlfriend
- unarguable proof of lesbian sexuality
- please the girl—her first true love
- forging into a sex life = being an adult

Cons:
- possible guilt upon eating
- possible traumatic flashback of cow and human flesh-dining images
- possible gateway activity to eating meat again

Three against four. The pros outweigh the cons.

She takes a deep breath, shifts her lips closer to her lover's edibles. Pubic hair tickles the tip of her nose. And a salty, musky, no, let's call it an *intoxicating*, scent plumes towards her face. A waft of something irresistible.

Yes, it's the scent that reels her in.

She decides: *As long as I do not chew on or swallow anything down here I will still be a vegetarian.*

Her tongue is there. Her mouth is there. And she begins to do to her girlfriend what she imagines would feel good to be done to her. Her girlfriend responds with gasps of positive feedback.

Yes, she's a natural at this.

There are more *mmmmms* escape from her girlfriend's mouth. Hips rock. Lips feel a sticky wet. Images of bitten flesh momentarily sprint across the stage of her mind. She quickly shuffles them to the wings, re-focuses on the actual stage-front matter, and continues to concentrate on the task at tongue.

Her girlfriend spasms.

Her girlfriend screams.

Her girlfriend emits a sound—animalistic.

Matchbooks, Pennies

Laramie, Wyoming. 1983. The fetus version of me pops out into the world, finally ready to graduate into an air-breathing baby version.

Pop.

Five years go by.

Kindergarten time.

Kids flock back to school, excited to be somewhere, have something to do other than feel the oppressive weight of utter boredom press down, hard, on their soft little kid bodies. It's a strong strand of boredom that invades this little town, a town that does not bustle like a cute little town can do. The desolate location-induced lethargy lingers, always; it won't give up, let up, won't stop hovering above the small kids, making them sick of playing kick-the-tumbleweed.

Once, I curved my kid body over the railing of a stairwell in my elementary school. This stunt led to the one and only time I have ever been yelled at by a teacher. I was sternly directed to *get down*. I also remember having a kindergarten-aged crush on this boy named Brian. Or was it Adam? Brandon? I don't know. I do know he had blonde hair and that we traded school pictures that year.

In my school picture that I traded with AdamBrianBrandon, I'm wearing my favorite outfit. My big head—all brown pig-tails and a mostly toothless, lopsided smile—sits perched atop my little body which is slightly slouched forward, but in its best outfit. The favorite outfit. The piece of clothing that consisted of exactly one piece of denim. A jean jumpsuit complete with long sleeves and long legs that suctioned to my arms and ankles with elastic cuffs. From crotch to neck there were plastic, opaque buttons, the color and shine that resembled the inside of a conch shell. Little circles of shiny swirls up the front of the jumper. An awkward floppy collar hung around the neck. So, we have a jean jumper with shell-like buttons and a floppy collar. Don't forget the pig-tails. And did I mention my two front teeth were missing, making big, goofy gaps the world could see each time I smiled? What really brought this outfit together, though, was a small, light blue hankie. Embroidered with one pink and green generic flower, the hankie demurely peeked up from the left breast pocket. Because this hodgepodge of an outfit was the only thing I ever wanted to wear, ever, I simply couldn't throw it away when it no longer fit. Currently, it is buried in a box somewhere in my mother's basement. Though I have the hankie sitting on my dresser.

Items stored in my mother's basement:
- Old school photos of her two daughters
- 15 years' worth of Jazzercise tapes used in order to learn the routines
- Christmas decorations

- My letter jacket from high school with a rainbow patch glued to it, because I thought it was funny to say I lettered in being gay
- A Foosball table
- Thanksgiving centerpieces made by my sister and me circa 1988
- Thick, twelve-inch long locks of curly brown hair from my major hair cut of 1999, wrapped in tin foil, stored away in the extra refrigerator
- An extra refrigerator
- Inherited tools my mother will never use
- A witch's hat
- The ashes of my dead father
- My favorite outfit from kindergarten

Since, as mentioned earlier, Laramie was an anti-bustling town, I had to provide my own entertainment. This is where each adventure began. Jean jumper uniform held my body, like getting a hug all over, all at once. What other outfits did I have? That's a damn good question. I don't know the answer, unless my memory actually is correct and I didn't move much in the world unless I was wearing my cherished, one continuous piece of denim clothing. The ways in which the elastic cuffs suctioned around my wrists and ankles made discovering the world a much more reckless (read: hella fun) act. The cuffs kept pebbles out. The denim shielded my skin from any sort of plant that would do something mean, violent, angry, to this skin.

Chelsey Clammer

Discovering the world, specifically my yard, again, always occurred with that outfit wrapped around me. There's a theme here. Please tell me you've picked up on it by now.

Behind our quaint, white house sat a small backyard full of lush trees and overgrown weeds. A forest to my child-sized self in which I could gleefully get lost. In stark contrast to this backyard jungle, the front yard consisted of brown bricks cemented around a random nut-bearing tree and a sandbox. Although the front yard was basically a blank space full of bricks, it was just as full of adventurous promises as its opposite, the backyard jungle. In such an open landscape, I could run around with the fantasies of solving crimes, accomplishing fantastic feats like saving my friends from danger, and digging deep into the sandbox to discover hard clumps I imagined to be dinosaur bones. In hindsight, I was terribly wrong about the dinosaur bones. Most likely, the sandbox clumps were chunks of the neighbor's cat shit. Like the tall, ensconcing trees that boarded me up in the backyard, there was also a high cement wall and iron gate that caged me in from the "traffic" on Kearney Street—which consisted of a few cars passing by at 25mph every two hours or so.

While the trees and cement wall kept me safe from the dangers of the larger world out there, my jean jumpsuit continued to shield my body from encroaching branches and biting ants that infected our yard. And yet, through all of these active scenes, the jumpsuit's hankie and dainty collar kept me feeling composed and mature. Imagine a mechanic in her grease-stained coveralls wearing a sleek, clean silk scarf around her sticky-sweaty neck. The hankie, while unnecessary, inspired in me a sense that I could be elegantly composed even in the midst of performing a dirty job, such as shoveling cat shit/dinosaur bones from my sandbox.

Items found in my dad's closet and garage a few days after his funeral:

- Business suits
- A dark wood box full of cuff links
- Two plastic boxes of Titleist golf balls, nine per box
- A wax-lined Albertson's paper bag containing three stale chocolate donuts
- A golf bag full of porn tapes
- Shoe polish (black)
- AA coins
- Empty bottles of vodka
- A broken gold Rolex watch
- A handwritten list that "Admitted to God, to ourselves, and to another human being the exact nature of our wrongs," as completed for the fifth step in Alcoholics Anonymous, which listed an item that confirmed my mother's twenty-year suspicion of an affair
- Various tools in two different conditions: rusted or still in the original packaging
- 17 books about the Civil War
- A black XXL-sized University of Colorado Boulder Buffaloes sweatshirt

When my father evicted himself from/vacated his life (some say suicide, some say accidental alcohol overdose, I say that either way a 0.46 blood alcohol level is quite impressive) he left the world as a drunk man, a father and husband with many forbidden secrets. I was twenty-one when my father died, and a few days after the funeral my mother enlisted me to help face the dirty job of sifting through the relics, which is to say his shit. My maternal grandparents also aided my mom in purging the house of his junk. It was hard to convince them to do so, as no one wanted to discover what this perma-intoxicated, secretive man kept hidden from the world. Such as a golf bag full of porn tapes. My grandfather discovered that one. But the job had to be done. Like my hankie did to my jumpsuit, I kept a small bit of composure in the face of this grimy job. I kept busy, calm, business-like as I focused on tasks and occasionally ordered my mother to do something when she sat staring at items that either a) she had never known he possessed, or b) reminded her too much of him. Neither of us cried. *Mom, throw away the cracked watch and donate the suits to the Goodwill. Mom, the tools can go to Rick. Mom, you'll never read about the Civil War, so add those books to the Goodwill pile.* I stayed steady, projected a sort of pseudo-halcyon while everything inside of me was earthquaking.

Seven years have slipped away since my mother found my dad dead, found him lying in a contorted position against the side of his bed. Since that morning of cracked ribs as she tried to revive him, regardless of the fact that his skin had grown stiff, hardened, gray, she has put 855 miles between her present, pleasant life and that old haunted house in Austin. Now living in Colorado Springs, she has found a life full of trails, trees, and freedom. Her current basement is a damp cement structure, good for swallowing painful reminders of her past. Such as her dead husband's ashes. They sit in a cardboard box. I'm curious about what this box is labeled. The box with my jean jumpsuit folded inside of it is labeled "Chelsey." But labeling the box containing my father's ashes with his name, "Jeff," is just too absurd to not be hilarious.

When my mother finally moved away from Austin after my father dude died, she lugged a bunch of boxes with her that contained our family's artifacts. She threw out a bunch of useless stuff, including old elementary school report cards, though she also kept a bunch of it, like the chunk of my hair from over a decade ago that is still wrapped in tin foil and is still residing inside of her extra refrigerator. She held onto the important things. The things that make our stories. Like an outfit that tells about my younger and more adventurous self. Like the exercise tapes that tell about a younger and more adventurous woman—my mother who taught Jazzercise for fifteen years. And while she held onto a lot of memory-inducing tchotchkes, she did slightly purge her possessions of a small amount of clutter that had accumulated over the years.

I recently moved into a new apartment, a one-bedroom that is all mine. My stuff has room to grow, to unfurl, a space in which more memories can accumulate. Here, I get to gain my own clutter that, at some point, meant something to me. One would think moving would be a great opportunity to throw out what isn't needed—a time when one can clear out stuff from a twenty-two-year-old version of me, and build on an opportunity to start anew. But I've never been able to let go. I can't relinquish what I might want to stumble across some day in the future. To forget that I kept _____, and now isn't it neat that I can hold _____ when I need to remember those past moments, memories. To continue to be who I am and whoever that will one day be. I can't stand to think that at some future point I'll be looking for that hankie from my kindergarten outfit, and realize I threw it out long ago. As a result of this, I end up moving a lot of unnecessary things, things that one might con-sider trash, yet things I consider to be important, things that move me from one life and into another, such as an old hankie.

When I finally unpacked my *fourteen* boxes of books (no lie), I came across Ali Liebegott's *The Beautifully Worthless.* After I finished reading it a few days later, I went back into my closet and started to unpack the clutter I moved with, throwing out the things that repre-sented not-that-important memories. I did this, because in the opening chapter of her book, Leibegott writes about a lonely woman wandering about the country in a beat-up truck, her dog as her companion. The book opens with the woman unpacking from her first move and discovering all of the junk she brought with her. She says, *"I can't stop dwelling on the fact that I moved a box filled with matchbooks and pennies. I wrote down on a slip of paper, 'matchbooks, pennies' and hung it on the wall so I wouldn't forget that I packed up the trash in my life and moved it with me to a new apartment."*

The trash I packed up from my old place and moved with me to my new apartment:

- A stack of letters from a roommate who eventually kicked me out because I kept drinking all of her liquor and never replaced it
- A baggie of dead batteries
- The remnants of burnt-down candles
- Shards of my favorite sushi plate
- A baggie full of twelve-inch long dreadlocks from when I trimmed them last year
- A duffel bag literally bursting at the seams with running medals
- Two 12-pound weights that are only ever lifted when moved from one apartment to another
- A bag of pillow stuffing larger than any pillow I own
- My dog's puppy teeth that fell out twelve years ago

Right now, I don't have a basement. I do, however, have a closet that recently experienced the death of its wire shelves. I was reading in my bed when I heard my memories collapse into a heap on the gray, carpeted floor. When I eventually fixed the shelves a few months later, I stowed away the things containing memories back into their resting place. I re-stacked my artifacts, wondering if one day I would sort through them and move some things into the clutter pile. Perhaps in a few years I won't need the XXL-sized University of Colorado Boulder Buffaloes sweatshirt to remember how my father spent his weekends drunk, in his room, screaming at the TV when the UC Buffs had an incomplete move (or something football-sounding of sorts). Because, perhaps at some point in my life, I'll be able to let go of it, will be able to live without it, like how I'm able to live without him.

Years from now when I complete my final move into some house I will choose to live in until I die, here are the things you will find in my future basement:

- A worn-out softball glove
- Books
- Old pictures of friends
- Coffee mugs
- A red hooded sweatshirt from my first swim team with my name (spelled correctly!) embroidered in white, cursive letters on the upper-left shoulder
- More books
- Candle holders sans burnt-down remnants of candles
- Matchbooks, pennies (because let's be real: Even with multiple possession-purges, there are some things of which I will never be able to completely let go)
- My father's XXL-sized University of Colorado Boulder Buffaloes sweatshirt that has not and never will fit me, but that my mother insisted I keep *to remember him*
- A hankie from my favorite outfit in kindergarten

Joe

I like pushing buttons.

I do not like clichéd figures of speech, an example of which could be, "I like pushing buttons."

A song I learned in third grade had a choreographed, chicken arm flapping dance to go along with it. There was a man in the song, Joe, whose boss told him one day to turn a button. Not press, mind you. But *turn*.

How exactly does one turn a button?

The song:

"Hello. My name is Joe. I got a wife, three kids and I work in a button factory. One day my boss says to me 'Are you busy?' I say no. He says 'Turn this button with your right hand," which was when Joe (us third graders) would start the movement of turning an imaginary button with our right hands. This movement would not cease until the song stopped.

The song continued:

"Hello. My name is Joe. I got a wife, three kids and I work in a button factory. One day my boss says to me 'Are you busy?' I say no. He says 'Turn this button with your left hand," which was when Joe (us third graders) would start the movement of turning an imaginary button with our left hands. This movement, along with the previously instructed turning of a button with our right hands, would not cease until the song stopped.

No one ever really knew how or when the song would stop.

"Now turn this button with your left knee." Then ankles. Then toes. And then, soon, the laughter that always burst when we ran out of appendages to employ for the job of turning imaginary buttons. Thus, the song continued in a creative way. One could call it absurd, actually.

"Now turn this button with your eyelashes." Then mouth. Then nose. Ears were the hardest. Our ability to turn multiple imaginary buttons with every bit of our anatomy finally ended when our uproarious, outrageous, unstoppable laughter kicked the shit out of our button-turning talents. Without fail, this always happened with the instruction of: "Now turn this button with your bottom."

Two questions:

1. What the fuck kind of buttons are they making in this factory?
2. Why was my third grade teacher making small children sing to, dance to and laugh at a song about oppressive workplace hierarchies?

Was she preparing us for the inevitable experience of working for some asshole who assigns asinine tasks to his employees, all of whom are underpaid?

As in: *We need to cut overhead costs. And since the factory workers appear to be turning buttons instead of making them, we must reduce their pay, as well as the number of employees we have in the button-creation department.*

And so the CEO massacres his workers' abilities to succeed at their jobs as he forces them to do odd and pointless things like turning buttons, just waiting for their production levels to drop. It's genius, really. Factory workers become fatigued by the extra button turning tasks said CEO demands of them, and so productivity declines, which then allows asshole CEO to fire them all because they are not "meeting the productivity standards as outlined in their job descriptions."

How perfect.

The CEO doesn't want to pay for unemployment.

Thus, fire 'em lazy bastards.

Joe has a wife and three kids.

When my husband and I lived in a small, mountain casino town for nine months, he was receiving fat unemployment checks while I gambled away all of the tips I made each day from my waitressing gig. Being a person who can get addicted to and fixated on anything that is a noun (in eighth grade I made curtains out of the hundreds of pop can tabs I had collected over the previous four years), gambling became my obsession—the clamor of dings and dongs so exciting, so encouraging to put more money into the slot machine because maybe, just maybe, this time the three red sevens will line up together on the middle line. *Fuck yeah!*

Slot machines no longer have levers to pull down in order to make the little numbers and symbols spin. Instead, they have buttons.

I like pushing buttons.

It's twenty-odd decades since the last time I sang and danced and laughed about oppressed factory workers. In these past years I have asked my friends if they knew this song. No one has ever answered yes.

Revelation: My third grade teacher's name was Mrs. Buttons.

Mrs. Buttons was terribly tyrannical, proven by the fact that when the end-of-school bell sounded she would make us stay seated until *she* said we could leave. Re: oppressive hierarchies. Thus, Mrs. Buttons was the first and only teacher I ever flipped off. She didn't like that. I couldn't help myself. Her nasally voice and garlic breath and holiday-themed, gaudy plastic brooches and blatant revulsion for all of us and the obvious hatred for her job really, I mean, like, *really, really, really*, pushed my buttons.

Your Lesbian Haircut

You're nineteen. It's a year after your first break up, after that raucous fight with your first girlfriend who is now standing above you with a razor in her hands. You are kneeling on the ground in front of her. And while she is your ex, she is still your friend because there are times when you need her, like how you need her right now. You need her right now, specifically, to shave your head.

She shaves your head, and good god thank you lordy jesus you finally feel butch. Like a real lesbian. Like a proud dyke with a shaved head.

You have finally decided to shave your head because the older woman you had a crush on, Jean, simultaneously broke your heart and pissed you off. This is how you rebel. This shaved head that you know Jean would hate. This shaved head that you actually love. Take that, bitch.

But you cannot get the thought of Jean out of your head. She stays inside your mind, picketing your therapist's healthy suggestion to *get over it already*. Because, months later, you are still wallowing in that beastly message you didn't think you'd ever hear, those last words she ever said to you:

You don't deserve for things to get better. Don't ever call me again.

WTF?!? You bitch.

You wish you could say this to her. But you know you won't.

Instead, you shave your head.

But even with your new peach-fuzzy 'do, her words still won't leave you. In fact, you're still trying to figure out what you did that pissed her off so much, that made her want to say a big "fuck you" to you. Was it because you never cleaned the stove? Or because her girlfriend was getting wicked jealous about how much time you were spending with Jean? Now you have this huge conspiracy about lesbian jealousy and how it makes you want to die.

Literally.

Jean's refusal to speak to you drives you crazy, makes you wicked mad. There's a double meaning there. You have been pushed out of the *we* that was comprised of you and Jean. You're nineteen and Jean's stoic silence drives you so nuts that you end up in a psych ward with a shaved head and a freshly pumped stomach. You're nineteen the first time you attempt suicide.

You did not write a note.

You wanted to shove Jean's face in the shit of silence.

In the psych ward, you meet Carol. Carol is quirkier than you. Carol is more fucked-up than you. Proof: Carol is married to one man, has a boyfriend, a girlfriend, too, and soon, in the psych ward, she starts to rub her hands all over your shaved head. When you are both released from the psych ward later on that week, Carol continues to rub your shaved head with her hands, only this time your shaved head is between her legs.

You're nineteen and take a semester off of college to be psych-ward-crazy and then learn the art of getting really drunk. Every night. And in the morning, too. Psych-ward-Carol and her boyfriend are always getting you really, really drunk. Always. You will remember the boyfriend's hot tub that the naked lot of you practically lived in, and you will also remember his pond with the canoe. You will not remember how to get to that house, because every time you drove out there you were stoned or drunk or both. Sometimes fucked up on coke. Or, twice, mushrooms. You do remember it was a pretty drive. But you will not remember being at home during that self-defined, student-status sabbatical. You suspect you never went home, because home was living with your parents. Fuck that. So for three months you lived with Carol and her boyfriend and her girlfriend, or, sometimes, her husband, too. Yes, you have three months to go wild before you have to re-domesticate your psycho mind to be an only slightly crazy college brain. You only kinda sorta do this. Because when you eventually, with great resistance, re-enroll to be an academic minion, you'll discover that pot makes every class better. So until that first day of class—that place where an enjoyable life goes to die—you drink as much Jack Daniels as you can stomach and sleep with Carol in every room and shower and position in her boyfriend's house which, you think, is somewhere in the woods.

You're nineteen. You do not hang out with your friends from college because you terrify them. They're afraid of getting to know you too well and, should you die, they would have to deal with all that grief. You're nineteen and all on your own except for these people in this house that is somewhere in the woods, maybe, and you fall asleep on a king-sized mattress with the thirty-four year old Carol and her fifty-two year old boyfriend who has eight fingers. You sleep a drunk sleep, and in the morning you wake up to the bed banging against the wall because he is banging her next to you in the bed. You are not a part of the we in those moments.

You wait until they are done with the banging, then you get up and go to the kitchen, open the bottle of Jack Daniels and drink what's left of it standing in front of the sink with your shaved head and your naked body. Then you go through another day of drinking with Carol to avoid the crazy that still crawls within you. Fuck you, Jean. You fall asleep not remembering what you did that day. Though you're not quite sure you ever really did anything, really, because you were really busy, what with the drinking and the fucking and what not. In fact, you won't remember much of this time, but the memories you will have will all consist of a king-sized bed, two ceiling fans whirring above your head, different bodies of water, the three of you doing some fantastic fucking on some really big, fat mattress, and that, before you passed out every night, you briefly wondered who, exactly, you were.

But when you woke up to your hangover and rubbed your hands all over your shaved head, trying to assuage that alcohol-pounding pain, the peach fuzz head told you who you were: the woman who got a lesbian haircut to rebel against the woman who drove her mad.

But no matter how many women you fuck, how many psych ward trips you take, and how many shots of whiskey you ingest, you cannot get the thought of Jean out of your (shaved) head. Regret occupies your mind. You wonder when you will acknowledge that you *are* out of your mind.

Hands

Your body tears, shatters.

You walk down a street at night, alone, and you are not thinking about him, the him who is behind you, the him you don't even know is there. And then you hear him. You hear his footsteps, running, and you assume they are the footsteps of a jogger. They are quickly approaching, and you step aside to let the late-night jogger slide past you. He does not slide past you. Instead, he grabs you from behind just as you approach the alley. He grasps your shoulder, grabs at what is under your skirt. You tear, shatter.

You fight him on the sidewalk, fight him past the darkness of the alley, fight him until he finally walks away. He finally walks away and you barely remain standing as you wait. You see his back, a black jacket and tan pants that will begin to look like every black jacket and tan pants you see on every man's body on every street near every alley. He walks down the sidewalk just past the alley, then turns around. Faces you. Turns back around and walks away. Turns around again, walks toward you, again, gets another look at what he controlled, corrupted, conquered, then turns away, again, head held up high. He leaves. He leaves several times, but he will always still be here. When he turns the corner, tucks his body around the brick building, you sob, collapse. Collapse in your torn skirt. Collapse into your own silent rage that wishes it had protected you. Wishes it had torn a part of him. Somehow you pick yourself up and continue your walk home, still sobbing, the strong part inside you still collapsing.

As you walk, you blame yourself for wearing this skirt, for walking home alone, for stepping aside instead of turning around when you heard feet running. You blame yourself for the part of you that is torn, shattered.

Now you watch him stagger down the hallway of your memory, watch him crash into your walls, smashing picture frames with his shoulders, leaving remnants of himself in the foyer. You trip over a small bit of the memory of him every day when you return home. An arm, a leg, a swath of his gelled, black hair. Sometimes his hands grab, again. Sometimes you struggle, again, to gain freedom. To repair what tore, shattered.

A year later, it will be new hands that repair, new hands that grab you safely from behind, new hands that hand back to you those torn and shattered parts.

There is a cross on the skin over her heart. She is not religious. The cross is more like an X, really, perhaps marking where it is she hopes for something to be found. The scar puckers up three inches above her pierced pink nipple, her slightly translucent and smooth flesh a stark backdrop to the gnarled, crossed tissue. Her skin is soft, but not innocent. She has marked herself many times. Cut. Slashed. You do not know what she has tried to guard her heart against. You have never asked why, why the X, why over her heart. You can make your assumptions. You can understand the need to feel something cut out of your skin, cut into your body.

You have asked her to grab you from behind. To plunge into you, to plunge into what it is you need to feel. You are aware that you might be triggered, that you might think of the man who grabbed you from behind a year ago. He did not plunge into you as hard as you want to feel her thumping inside of you. Maybe her pounding will relieve the pressure that has been building at the base of your back, growing with its silent anger and rage. You need her to release the clenched-up part of you, the anxious part from where terror gripped you tight once his hands gripped you.

She straps on the appendage. Spare Parts, the brand name of the dildo and harness. You watch her hands fondle the straps and silicone mass, and adjust it all to fit her slim hips. Her green Mohawk spikes upward from her smiling face. Her safe face. Her face of solace. You have requested the lights to be on, because you do not want to lose yourself in the dark. You want to see everything in front of you, the maroon pillow, the teddy bear grabbing a plush "I love you" heart, the periwinkle walls with pictures of smiling faces hanging on them. You feel her kneeling behind you, ready for you, ready for the possibilities of your reaction. Ecstasy, shuddering, screaming, terror. A combination of all of these things.

You are prepared to tremble in whatever way your body needs to tremble. To tear and shatter, if need be.

The quality of her hands makes what feels raw and tender lean towards comfort. The tendons of her palms form themselves around the angles of your hips as you wait expectantly for her to push inside of you. You can feel the two, hard metal rings that decorate her fingers against your hips. An anchor on one, thick ring circles her middle finger; the other piece of metal on her index finger bears the word "cunt." You need these fingers to grasp and control your own cunt. To anchor you. She asks if you are ready, and as you brace your knees and hands on the sinking mattress, you nod your head, *yes*. She enters. She steadies her own rhythm and begins to guide you. At first, you are not enjoying this. You know you will not come, but you need this. An orgasm was never the point. The point is to feel, to feel her hands, to feel her hands grabbing you from behind.

You fall into her. Your hips buck and rise, but she holds you steady. Controls you with her hands. You begin to release just a bit, begin to let your body be wrought by someone else. Conceding to her hands gives you a respite from trying to protect that wound-up part of you. You do not know how this is possible. How it is that your body trembles in the same way from two different types of hands grabbing you from behind. His terrorizing hands versus her intoxicating ones. But you tremble anyway, and something leaves you. You cannot tell what it is that has left. You assume it might be his hands.

Later, in her bathroom, you wipe yourself clean and see the sign hanging above her sink. "The world is waiting to hear your story," it says. And it is true. You are finally back in the world, waiting for your story to emerge, to hear what it is that needs to be said. To hear that shift away from the sounds of shattering, to hear the new sounds of stories being spoken, new sounds that need to be heard, that must be heard by the world. You need the stories in order to name, to control, to conquer the feeling of shattered and torn. You want to speak, but you are still trying to find your voice. Months after this, she tells you she wants to start writing again. That she was looking through her journals, sifting through the pages with her ringed anchor and cunt fingers, and on every page she found details of her sexual adventures. That is what she wants to write about. You wonder if she will write about you. You wonder if the world is ready to hear that story.

Sarah

White furniture surrounded me. I knelt on the floor, immersed in heavy sobs. My knees pressed into my roommate's ugly and expensive oriental rug. Snot heaved onto its red and green pattern—the soft yellows did nothing to hide the globs of mucus. Sunlight streamed in through the large front windows of that condo. It was not my condo. It was my roommate's condo. She was crazy and decided to let me stay there. She was crazy because she was actually crazy. Like, crazy, crazy. Like me, crazy. But she was also crazy because she was letting me live there. I was a hot mess. Bulimic, alcoholic, self-mutilating, and generally just falling into pieces.

Literally falling into pieces on the ugly red and green Persian rug in that too-white condo. My roommate was away for the weekend. She was the woman who would later give me a blue nylon running jacket and say, "Funny. This is the jacket I attempted suicide in last year." I've attempted suicide before, but I have never tried to hand off the clothes I was wearing at the time.

But this wasn't about her and her white furniture or her ugly rug. I didn't care about her rug. I was too con-sumed by my own problems to wonder why she wanted to own that rug. The problems included binging and purging three times that day. And it was only 10am. And that was not unusual for me. I purged the cereal, the ice cream, the two pizzas, and the mashed potatoes. But then, in some moment of post-puking clarity, I decided to call a friend who was just as lonely in life as I was. This is why we were friends. Neither of us really had any friends, so we befriended one another to help each other through the hard shit.

This was the hard shit. And in that random flash of clarity, I dug my cell phone out of my pocket and called her.

Sarah, I can't stop puking. I cried and I hollered. And she just listened. She told me to breathe. And so I tried that. She told me to breathe again, and that time I really did it. My stomach crackled with each breath.

I was binging and purging because I did not know what else to do. There were no friends because of my craziness, there was an ocean of course work for grad school classes, work was a mess. I was an AmeriCorps volunteer. Pay was only $5.50 an hour, so it was basically volunteer work. And it was stressful work. I spent my days at a high school where violence was the theme. The peer mediation program was a joke to the students. The gang members didn't want to talk out their problems. They just wanted to fight. And my mediators were the kids with no friends, the ones who came into my office during their lunch hour for training in order to be mediators. They didn't want to be in the cafeteria, because the other kids always threw food at them. So they came into my office each Tuesday and Thursday and munched away at their candy, the sugar that sustained them throughout the day. They had their social anxiety problems. They had their acne. They had their reasons to not exist anymore. I could relate to them, their desires to disappear, their unsatisfying lives. My life was a constant hangover; the school had cavernous halls with the depressing dark green paint that was chipping off onto the black-painted floors. And yet my job was to guide these youth, to show them that talking out their problems would help to heal their school, their community, themselves.

Two years of therapy, and still cutting my arms, no necessary weight gain, utter anxiety from being sexually groped by a stranger. He had run up behind me and grabbed my shoulder, then stuck his hand up my dress. There was therapy for that assault, to try and get over it, but the therapy was just palliative, just a tool to try and feel a connection with someone once a week. Plus, it was at least one hour a week not puking. That was all I had. Yet each day got worse. Drinking, cutting, puking. This was perhaps why all of my friends left me: The level of scariness heightened each day. Each Wednesday night after therapy I got drunk, again, continued to spend all of my money on booze and then dumpster-dove my way home in search of food to binge and purge on until I fell into a sloppy, mucus-covered heap on my bed. The next mornings were: hungover as hell with a sore throat and bloated stomach, problems of troubled teens. Nothing there was working.

It was a Saturday morning when I called Sarah. I just knew that I needed her voice, needed someone who could take care of what was no longer being taken care of. There was no expectation, but something to get me off of that ugly carpet in the glaring sun and off to do something productive with my life. Snot ran down my chin. My jaw was sore; my stomach felt as if it was exploding and bleeding all over itself. My throat was gunked up with mucus. There was no breath, just sobbing.

All these things were incredibly ugly. Not just with the havoc the drinking and the puking wreaked on my skin and my face, or the scars that accumulated on my forearms, but the level of concealment hiding these things was disgusting, too. There was constant anxiety about trying to hide from my friends the copious amount of liquor consumed each night, because they already thought I drank too much. There was nervousness about hiding the puking from my friends, about concealing that nasty disorder so they wouldn't be disgusted by me. All of this hiding made me anxious. That was what my therapist said. There was the trauma of being assaulted, and also dealing with the anxiety about those addictions, about the hiding of drinking, puking, cutting from my friends. I didn't want to be revealed. There were three things I knew that would momentarily alleviate the anxiety—drinking, purging, cutting. Anxiety over the addictions, using the addictions to quell the anxiety. The cycle continued. But my therapist knew what to do with me. I needed to get out of that trap; there were "tools," she said, to break through that cycle. The "toolbox" was hidden inside of me.

Another thing that was not working was the MA in Women's Studies I was working towards. I studied women like me, studied the reasons these things happen, the societal pressures, the culturally imposed self-images that were impossible to live up to. You would have thought someone with my background would never find herself in a place like this, and if she did, she would know how to "thrive." "Thrive" was another thing my therapist said. But even completing an MA in Women's Studies, even working part-time at a feminist bookstore, even in therapy with a feminist relational therapist, there was an eating disorder, one that was tearing my body apart. I even had a theoretical paper on eating disorders and alcoholism to write for my Women's Studies program, muted with my own eating disorder and my own alcoholism. Thinking about it didn't help. Putting it into academic jargon didn't help. Nothing helped.

There was feminist strength inside of me; my body was beautiful just the way it was, but I failed to feel it, failed trying to will it to be true. My therapist directed: self-love. Compassion. She said I needed to recognize the strength and beauty within myself. And while I wanted to agree with her, wanted to think all of those beautiful things about myself, what I felt was horrible and ugly and thirsty for another drink. That drink, that mound of food to shove inside of myself in order to push away all of that atrocious anxiety. My feminist relational therapist had faith in me. The only feminist thing going on there was having a strong woman support me. Sarah was on the phone with me. She was there for me.

Sarah cared. There was no reason for her to care, but she did. I did not care about myself, but there was someone who did. She told me to breathe again. She asked me what had been going on, why there was so much puke that day, if I was sick and needed to go to the hospital. Should I tell her the truth?

Sarah was a volunteer at the feminist bookstore. Sarah helped to put out the metal folding chairs for each event, helped to clean up the store afterward of the spilled red wine and crumbs of yellow crackers and smears of white cheese. She had an ability to give. She was a volunteer and did all of the work without pay, and with a kind and generous smile.

A few months before that telephone call on the ugly rug, Sarah was cleaning the store after an event while I counted the money. When our duties were done, I asked Sarah if she wanted to go out for a drink. My girlfriend, Jen, was slowly slipping out of my life, all of my friends had also started to retreat, and I needed a new drinking buddy, someone who would also spend her nights avoiding her problems with alcohol. She agreed to come with me, but instead of pretending everything was fine in our lives, we opened up to each other because our problems had been pressing on our sternums. We needed to exhale them out of our lungs.

Sarah had an interesting relationship with her family, one that was causing her much stress. My relationships with my friends were fading, causing me much stress. We talked about our relationships as I finished my third drink and she began working on her second. Her brown eyes looked thoughtfully into my hazy hazel ones through her small, wire-rimmed glasses. She looked at my empty glass and ruffled her short, curly brown hair with her thick, pale fingers. As we started to sip at our new round of drinks, we each shifted our wildly different body weights on our bar chairs. Sarah was short and stocky; I was much taller and too-lean. And though my bulimic face was twice the size of Sarah's triangular skull, she did not comment on the bloatedness. Because while in that dark bar, with the fancy cocktails and the imported beer, I told her how Jen left me, how she said goodbye, how it devastated me, but not about the main problem, which was swallowing food and then immediately puking it back up. I considered for a second if I would tell her this, decided no, not now, and finished my fifth drink.

I hid the facts of my bulimia in hopes that Sarah's care would continue, that she wouldn't get scared away like the others. I was ugly when I puked—the puffy face, the blood vessels that burst in my eyes, the glands in my neck too swollen. No one wanted to stand around and witness it. What I did tell Sarah that night was about the cutting, and she had already started to see the drinking. She would soon witness the drinking each night, would always be astonished by the amount of liquor I could consume. For some reason the cuts didn't astonish her, didn't make her eyes widen or her face turn. She simply noted them and listened. She did not know where my pain came from, what would make me cut, but she understood the serious- ness of it and did not retreat away from me that night or any night after it. What she also didn't know during our first drinking date was that when I ate the chips and guacamole with her in my drunk, care-free attitude, I was only able to do so because I excused myself to the bathroom, and easily heaved it out in one backwards gulp.

Then there was more alcohol, to replace the liquor that had been thrown up along with the food.

Maybe she knew these things. Maybe she sensed it, then, figured it out by looking at my red, wet eyes returning from the one-stall bathroom. Blood vessels on the verge of bursting. Maybe she cared too much to say anything, sensed this newly-arising friendship would only last if we first kept quiet about what could create judgment. It was in that silence there was caring, in that she didn't point out what was obvious, that she didn't embarrass me that night by noting what she had to have known. She kept quiet about those things, saved me from the embarrassment, and allowed for me to figure out how to move past them on my own.

Then, a few months later, on my knees on that ugly carpet, with the stark white furniture and white walls spotlighting and echoing the sounds of my desperation, Sarah used her voice to soothe me. After the few breaths choked into my lungs, I told her I did not want to do this anymore. *Do what?* Detour to the story about how I lost my girlfriend, Jen, lost all of the friends who used to give me support because of the cutting. *Because I'm disgusting.* Confession. She asked why I thought I was disgusting, and I wavered for a second as I decided whether I should or should not reveal my bulimia secret. There were the things, the ugly facts of the addictions, the secrets that could not be shared with anyone because of embarrassment.

Like, bulimia gave me great abs.

I tried to appreciate the small things in life. Like how Sarah didn't ask me on the phone, right then, what I had done the previous night after the bar.

I had walked down the alleys on my route home from the bar and looked in each dumpster for food—any food—to eat. Dumpsters are all the same: big, green, metal rectangular bins with the black plastic lids. The insides of them always feel oily, always have the grease and grime from other people's discards. They all smell the same. All human trash has a sweetly sour and rank smell, a mustiness. The stale loaves of bread absorbed that smell. The scent of trash soaked up into the bread. There was also the endless clumps of stale pizzas in the dumpsters near the college campus and disregarded take-out left-overs with this smell.

I have been a vegetarian since I was fifteen, and then, a decade later, still tried to keep up with that diet as I dove for my food, which was utterly unnecessary because I would immediately throw up all of what I just ate. Somewhere in my mind was the vegetarianism. If I set out rules for what I ate, then maybe I would start to eat regularly again. Or perhaps this was just control over another facet of my diet. During one of my first dumpster-diving sprees, I realized I was powerless to the thought of controlling what I ate. And, though I was tempted, I did not eat the hamburgers, but eventually disregarded my non-animal diet, finding the remains of a pizza with pepperoni. I didn't try to pick off the stale bits of meat; I was going to throw it up anyway, what difference would it make what was swallowed?

Chelsey Clammer

The night before the call to Sarah on the ugly rug, I had left her at a bar and had gone down the alley looking for food. My eyes had almost adjusted to the yellow street-light hue as I tried to decipher if there was any food in each white bag of trash. But my drunk eyes played tricks on me. I accidentally ripped open a bag of shit-filled cat litter.

As I hopped between each dumpster, filling my stomach with smelly food, a black man with gray, wiry hairs sticking up from his beard saw me and asked if I needed a place to stay. His eyes looked tired, wrinkled, like he had experienced too much life, but in those old eyes, kindness for me. For a brief second, I saw myself through this elderly man's eyes. With my dreadlocks and trash-stinking clothes, with a look of lost desperation, of having nothing to keep me tied to this world, I must have looked like a homeless child, like a teen who had given up hope, who had nowhere to go.

But there was my roommate's too-white condo to go home to. And what this man did not know was that I was there because my bloated stomach was raging, because I needed something to soak up the odious amount of liquor. Anything to stave off the alcohol poisoning. My body tried to survive itself.

Once the old man was out of my view, there was feasting, again, on the discarded food

I was stuffed and nauseous with trash chemicals and the lingering liquor by the time I returned home. I took a plastic grocery bag and up-chucked the food consumed. I knelt in my closet in an attempt to muffle the sounds from my roommate who slept down the hall. This is how I hid my bulimia. The quiet heaves, the throwing up when she was asleep.

My roommate never woke up. Sarah asked nothing about what happened after the bar.

Sarah's silence came from a place of caring. But my roommate's silence, the silence about why our bathroom sink was clogged up with the black gunk of old, chewed-up food, felt different. The bathroom sink was another place to dispel my binged food. If, after flushing the toilet of vomit, I stood up and felt there was still more in me that needed to be expelled, then there was the sink. Thus, the toilet flushed only once, like I was just peeing. And while my roommate's silence did nothing to stop me from doing this, I, in a way, appreciated it. That was my mask of normalcy, the silence that kept me looking sane.

But then, on the phone, Sarah was trying to break that silence. She was trying to get me to admit all that I was hiding. On the phone, I did not tell Sarah about the drunk dumpster diving from the night before. But I did finally say it, finally let the words crack through my teeth, my rotted gums, the words spilled out of me like partly digested food. *I'm bulimic.*

A month before this phone call, Sarah took a picture of me in Michigan on the lake. It was sunset, and my dreads waved in front of the pink winter sun. Ice and snow consumed the beach, and the sun hung low against them. With my back bent forward, my long dreads hung down and covered my face. They were a curtain for the sun; the light highlighted and surrounded each dread. Looking back on this picture, this is a metaphor for something, something about how good it was to finally have a friend, to have someone who had my back, who stood behind me and helped me to shine. But it wasn't that simple, especially when one of us was hiding.

We went on a weekend vacation to Michigan on the same weekend I had gone away to Madison with my girlfriend Jen the year before. Jen and I were in love, then, a strong love that showed no hints of going away. In the year that had passed, there was so much loss: Jen to my addictions, all of my friends because of the bulimia and hiding. But they knew. There's no way they could have not known. But no one wanted to talk about it, and so they turned their backs and ran. I don't blame them; I would have done the same. But then there came Sarah to catch me, to not run, to understand me, to not judge, but to help me do more than just barely survive.

She came with me to Michigan to keep me company, to drink wine and shut ourselves off from the cold air in the warm cabin with books. We drank and we ate, and when Sarah ventured off to the store down the road for more wine, I ate a few pieces of bread with some butter then threw them up in the bathroom. I did not binge, but I needed that feeling of purging in order to get the memories of Jen out of my system, the feeling of her that had been pressing in my bones. Sarah soon returned with more red wine, and I wondered if she knew that I had thrown up, if, again, she could see it on my face. She said nothing, poured me another drink, and we sat back in our conversation, continued to learn who one another was, staying silent about the one thing that screamed.

Her silence was caring.

Before the phone call on the rug, when we first entered into our friendship, Sarah tried to understand my other addictions. She tried to understand them so well that she almost hurt herself trying. She wanted to understand the cuts, to see if a physical pain could really help to relieve an emotional one. One night at the bar, she told me about her experiment that day. This was a month before the Michigan trip and just a few weeks after we had started to become friends. A few nights earlier I had shared with her an essay I had written about cutting. She wanted to understand. A few days later, while she was at work, she felt frustrated and overwhelmed, she said. She closed her office door, shut herself off from the world. She hiked up one leg of her brown, stretchy pants. She took a plastic twisty tie from off the end of a loaf of bread, and tried to dig into the pale, plump skin. A subtle scratch that got her nowhere, something that irritated the skin rather than bringing her any relief. But she was trying to understand.

Before she met me at the bar that night, she confessed her actions in therapy. As she told me about what she did with the twisty tie, I wondered what her therapist thought of me, that crazy friend, a bad influence. I was not responsible for Sarah's actions. She described the incident, her thoughtful words that were silent about blaming me. It was not my fault. My vodka soda reached up to my lips. One distorted thought made me smile—I was the crazier one. My crazy antics were somehow better than hers, crazier than hers. I had the win here; the thick scars on my arms were proof that I was better at self-mutilation. I knocked back those crazy thoughts with another drink, and smiled instead at this friend. Because, unlike the people who had left me, Sarah was trying to understand.

I'm bulimic.

Yeah, I know, she said in her soft voice.

And suddenly the stark white of the apartment didn't feel so threatening, so wanting to cast me out of its purity. Someone knew. And still cared.

My breath felt lighter. And my stomach no longer crackled. And with this admission the puking stopped. The binging, the drinking stopped, the cutting stopped.

That is not how it worked.

A year later, Sarah is the one who finally took me to the emergency room. The night before she took me to that emergency room was a night of drinking away all of my money and taking one last trip home through the dumpsters. There was the nightly routine of eating and puking, getting all of the fierce liquor and smelly food out of me by puking. By then, I lived on my own, as my crazy roommate with the ugly rug and the too-white furniture kicked me out because I was binging and purging all her food. She caught me one morning before I could walk to the store and replenish the refrigerator. And so she kicked me and my addictions out. On my own, it got even worse. Though, with my confession to Sarah that one Saturday afternoon a year before, I thought that was it. The secret was expelled from my body, and I thought I would stop expelling the food. But it had been a year, and, still, there was puking. Sarah knew this, knew what happened after the bar each night, and yet she still did not judge, still only wished me well and told me to call her if I needed anything.

Now, a year after the bulimic admission and another morning after a night of drinking and puking, I needed her, again. I needed her quiet voice, the way she let air hang between each thought. Needed her thoroughness, the way she considered each phrase, each action. The way she did not judge. I needed her to keep me from disappearing. And, she had a car, so I needed her to take me to the hospital.

My arm was bleeding. I cut it again, as cutting continued to be a part of my nightly ritual, something to go along with the drinking and the puking. Sarah knew this, knew how the cutting didn't actually hurt me, but the consequences of it did. The friends who ran away when the cutting got deep, the girlfriend who left because she couldn't stand my scars.

I called Sarah again, only this time holding my arm, trying to affix a bandage. She knew the gravity, could hear it in my voice. Five minutes later she was at the apartment. She showed up with a tentative smile, not knowing what mood I was in. I smiled back at her, letting her know that I would be okay, now that I was leaving, getting out of the apartment that trapped me with the drinking, the cutting, and the puking. Off to the hospital for stitches, then off to the psych ward to have experienced professionals take care of me. To get the alcohol out of my system, to try and have a normal eating schedule without binging and purging. To let my cuts heal.

In the car as we drove north towards the hospital, Sarah did not ask about this, did not question if the hospital was really where I wanted to end up. She was silent, perhaps because, by then, she was getting a little exasperated with supporting me, her being my only friend. Perhaps she needed the break from me more than I needed it from myself. If this was true, she said nothing to me in that car ride, but silently drove me to the hospital. My stomach hurt and I was horribly hung over.

She saw me to the waiting room, sat there while the triage nurse asked me the questions. *Why are you here? How old are these cuts? Are you suicidal?* Soon, I was in a room and I had a guard outside of my door. There was nothing in this room that could hurt me, just Sarah who kept me company. The pale yellow walls, the peach-colored bed, the gray chair that Sarah sat in, all comforted me. She leaned back in her gray, padded chair and we began joking about something, god knows what, but smart little quips about life and the hospital and the cuts that got me to laugh. Sarah cared for me in the only way a best friend could, by letting me make my own mistakes, and being there to drive me to the hospital.

After the stitches, and after an hour of waiting for the social worker to come and assess me, Sarah took off. She had her own life to live and there was nothing else she could do for me when the professionals swooped in. I would not see her for ten days. In that emergency room, I did not know that I would stay in the psych ward for a week and a half, that I would call Sarah every day because the nurses took my cell phone away and hers was the only number I had memorized. She, again, would talk with me on the phone, again would get me back into myself with each considerate word. I would come out of that psych ward and never drink again, and I would finally begin to heal. Sarah would help me through that, too. She was the one who brought me to the hospital, and she would be the one who would be there for me when I reemerged. She would drive me back home and continue to stay with me, to help me clean up my house of the liquor bottles and rusty razors. She continued to be my friend as I learned how to be one for myself.

Seven

With seven miles left to run in this fifty-mile race, my legs still trot along at a relatively fast pace. An enormous Wisconsin forest—host to fifty ultramarathon runners today—has a soft, single-track, dirt-packed trail the lot of us will follow until we pass that finishing line, hours from now. My pace is relatively fast—as fast as it can be for someone approaching mile forty-three.

While the trees are not rushing past me in a whirl, I'm at least not dragging my feet through the vague mud. The race started with an annoying drizzle, but six hours later the trail is considering becoming dry. Deeper into the forest, a tall quilt of leaves blocks the ground from the warming sun. Keep shuffle shuffle shuffling feet along the damp ground, and avoid the presence of physical pain by getting lost in dreams and memories.

Thoughts of you enter me, always, but become even more alive when my legs and body and blood and lungs run long distances. Always. You. I want you here. Trotting along life next to me. You, who are not my recent ex-girlfriend, and I'm very happy about that. I don't like her. Never really did. You are a woman who could never be defined as boring. Unlike my recent ex-girlfriend, who shoved our sex life and every facet of the life we shared into a lockbox, labeled that ugly metal thing "us," eviscerated the key with her freaky mental powers that had the ability to blast enjoyment out of *anything*, chucked the lockbox in the freezer just to make sure nothing—like love, like my willpower to break up with her—grew, the you who I imagine running next to me is a you who has a personality, one I would enjoy hooking up with, one that could jump-start our conversations, our connection. Right now, my fantasies of you escort me down the course, help me to labyrinth around the forest, to navigate the trail of my own thoughts. To keep me going.

This Wisconsin forest is not, obviously, the Colorado forest the seven-year-old me explored during those formative growing-up years. Here, in this Wisconsin forest, there are no pine trees, deer antlers, bowling pins, or large rolls of Astroturf. This present-day forest, in which a sizable collection of passionate runners meander about for eight hours and then some, seems more mature than my kid-wandering forest. This one is composed of towering oaks and zen-inducing single-track trails. It's not host to a short, bush-like pine tree mini-forest where a young girl wanders about her self-proclaimed "Smurf Forest" in the afternoons out of a lack of anything else to do in a tiny Colorado town. However, both forests hold fantasies about desire.

- Colorado, 1990
    - Found objects
        - Bowling pin
        - Astroturf
            - (for reals)

Chelsey Clammer

- Wisconsin, 2009
  - ○ Found relationship
    - ▪ You
      - (in my head)

The magic of many trees gathered together, in one spot, right here.

Because this is about imagination, surprises, discovery. It's about being open to considering what could be. Such as intriguing, out-of-place objects. Such as searching for—and finding—you. Uncovering odd objects called me back to that forest almost every afternoon, just to wander about with an open mind that was ready to find anything. Nineteen years later, the desire for discovery unfurls within me. It's what brought you here, to my head, in this small section of Wisconsin land I twirl my body around. I speak to you out loud, the you who I desire to be here, with me, right now.

I make eyes at you—flirtatious eyes that glance in your direction, as if you are here, running next to me. An hour passes. Two miles to go. We've been talking to each other for over ten miles now, and this realization makes me wonder if my sanity actually is slowly breaking down into delusions as my body continues to tire. Run long enough, and you'll start to hallucinate, because the body starts to break down, which makes the mind trip over sanity quite a bit. Part of me wants this to happen, to have whole body hallucinations, each vision insistent on fulfilling my desires for you to be here with me, running and talking and breathing and laughing.

"What trail does the crazy runner take?" You coyly ask.

"I don't know."

"The psychopath."

The you who is not a runner, and thus would never accompany me on this journey, is now pushing chopped bits of laughter into my ears. It's a laugh no one else hears. It's a laugh that keeps my legs moving, keeps me distracted with a desire that spreads through my physical self.

Through your laughter and my increasingly delusional mind, I glide further into that zone of unconstrained mental space. My mind explores a landscape of thoughts I wouldn't have the space to traverse if my body never wandered around sections of nature. This mental release is familiar. I've felt it since I was seven, since I first experienced how the wide area of a forest could expand my mind as my body entered into a space of movement, of freedom.

In Colorado, I walked through the forest alone.

In Colorado, I walked through the forest alone.

In the early 1990s, my family lived in Elizabeth, Colorado. Elizabeth is a town no one has ever heard of. A tiny town—one paved road, no stoplights. One high school, one middle school, one elementary school. A downtown composed of three businesses: the movie store, the toy store, the barber. A small corner market where one could buy bruised fruit. We never shopped there. Instead, my mom would make the forty-five minute drive every week to the Safeway two towns over in order to get groceries. Anything we did or needed was a forty-five minute drive away. Swim practice, school supplies, piano lessons. Milk, gas, light bulbs. Necessities. The way out of Elizabeth to get on that forty-five minute drive was down the one paved road that eventually stretched over to Franktown, then, ten minutes later, to Castle Rock (behold! Safeway!). The paved road went up and down, up and down, up and down some small hills as it unfurled away from Elizabeth and ran past small patches of forests connected by farms, the landscape decorated with farmhouses, more trees, gates, fake deer lawn ornaments, American flags, real deer, plenty of dead squirrels, dead rabbits, dead skunks, and occasionally a dead dog or two.

Forty-five minutes of this view that connected Elizabeth to the rest of the world was a normal part of our lives. Because that's just the way things were in Elizabeth; residents exchanged convenience for the beautiful horizon of trees and towering mountains. Living forty-five minutes away from everything was an inevitable aspect of living in the forest-filled, Colorado country.

Eventually, my family moved to Texas and, at twenty-three, my now ex-girlfriend—we'll call her Angie –and I would take road trips from Austin to Colorado a few times a year. The drive was about twelve to fourteen hours, depending on visibility and guts to go over the speed limit. Most of the drive was through West Texas. There is nothing in West Texas but more of Texas. Dry. Flat. Brown. A handful of tiny, dusty towns littered the paved road on which we drove to get to the mountains. That paved road was the asphalt river from which each town's one paved road with its one lonely stoplight branched off. Amarillo, the northernmost town in Texas, was each road trip's smiling point. Seven hours into the thirteen-ish hour drive from Austin to Colorado, you hit Amarillo, the halfway point in one's escape from Texas. The first time we made this trip and were celebrating our almost-departure from Texas via Amarillo, I commented, "Dang, Angie. We should live in Amarillo. Colorado's only six hours away. We could make weekend trips!"

"Chelsey, when you live in Amarillo, everything is six hours away."

She had a point.

While, as a kid, I quickly became accustomed to how everything was forty-five minutes of an arm's reach away, six hours would be a bit trying. Besides, Elizabeth had that horizon one fell in love with. Everything in Amarillo was painted with a hue of desiccated gray and adorned with tumbleweeds. Passing through the last Texas town made me appreciate that, while it took forty-five minutes to pick up some Q-tips, Elizabeth provided a landscape on which beauty unleashed itself.

In Colorado, I walked through the forest alone.

Angie could never remember the chronology of her life. Did she date Billy when she was twelve or when she was fourteen? Did Nana die when she was ten or thirteen? I, on the other hand, have always known the timeline of my life and can usually pinpoint an event to within six months of its actual occurrence.

Angie's lack of a memory was not something I found cute, as our conversations about the past were very frustrating.

"How old were you when you dated Billy?"

"Um," she bit her lip, "I don't remember?"

"Who was your teacher in school?"

"What does my teacher have to do with Billy?"

"We're trying to create a sense of time, Angie. If you can remember your teacher, we can figure out what grade you were in, and then know about how old you were."

"Oh. Um. I don't know? I didn't have any classes with Billy."

I knew I could push her. I could ask her what classes she had that Billy was not in. Maybe then she would at least remember that she had classes that had teachers who taught specific grades. Or, another memory-sparker: Did she have any major haircuts in high school? Did this Billy person tuck long blonde hair behind her ear, or did he grab on tight to short, red highlights?

Ultimately, I didn't really care how old she was when she dated Billy. From her stories about him, he seemed like an asshole. Plus, I was sliding out of love with her as fast as I had slipped into it. Perhaps this decreasing love was because our brains didn't recall the world in the same way.

I'm assuming she was thirteen, mostly because no one wants to remember the awkward age of thirteen.

Questions I ask myself in order to figure out how old I was when something happened in my life:

1. Where was I living?
2. Who was my teacher?
3. How long was my hair?
4. Was I hot or cold?

For example:

"How old were you when you first thought you were gay?"

1. I was living in Elizabeth, Colorado, when I imagined cuddling with a famous actress in order to feel happy and get to sleep.
2. Ms. Gray was my teacher at the time, and I remember this because I had a crush on her, too. And I would also think about her as I walked alone through the forest out back behind my house. So it was 2nd grade.
3. My hair was short and did not tickle my eyes when lying in bed dreaming about older women kissing my forehead. So that must have been the first half of 2nd grade when I cut my hair the summer immediately before, because I got sap in it one day while walking through the aforementioned forest —which is quickly becoming the leading role of this essay—and decided to cut it short instead of trying to wash it out.

4. I was wrapped up in a lot of blankets when I had those fantasies about those women, because it was cold. So it must have been in November or December.

Thus:

There was a time when I would fall asleep, wrapped up in blankets and dreaming about Murphy Brown/Ms. Gray holding me close and kissing my forehead, my forehead as it was framed by my short hair. This thought soothed me happily to sleep. And thus, the first indication of my big gayness was in the late fall or early winter of 1990, when I was seven-and-a-half years old.

Maybe all of this is to say I have a good memory.

Or, that I have liked to cuddle with women for a long time.

Here's my forehead, beautiful lady. Have at it.

In Colorado, I **walked** through the forest alone.

I'm running my first fifty-mile race. This one is in Texas and it's a few years after the break-up between the Angie and me. Now, I'm good and addicted to the feeling of moving my body for eight hours, mostly because I crave that head space. Angie despised the fact that I ran long distances. She couldn't understand why I would want to spend three to five hours every Sunday morning running by myself rather than being around her. It was a valid question, one to which I only ever gave a half-assed answer.

"It's not that I don't want to spend time with you, Angie, it's just that I love running, and I can only ever do my long runs on weekend mornings."

"But don't you love me?" An irritating, yet valid, question.

"But Angie, I never question why you spend eight hours every day reading philosophy rather than spending your time talking with me." She shoots for deflecting and scores! Master of redirecting, yes I am.

This conversation has stuck in my head for the post-breakup three years, because it wasn't a rarity. One could call it a standard, actually. In fact, it was a weekly event for each of those four years in which we dated. That's a lot of personal space defense.

Because, ultimately, the space is what it was about. I needed that space. And it wasn't just the space of running eighteen to fifty miles to get away from Angie for a few hours, but for the well-being of my own psyche. Gotta get that body out into those locations that were relatively uninhabited. Gotta get that space in order to think, to dream. Not a lot of people understand this, especially, obviously, Angie.

One question people inevitably ask when I tell them I run ultramarathons: "What do you think about when you run for that long?"

I vague some answers, such as I sing to myself, or I just zone out. Or whatever. I don't know. What the fuck do you think about for eight hours? The real reason is a fantasy that will go unspoken. The ladies. The ways in which I (in)voluntarily run around the city with a woman of who I am totally crushed out on and have conversations with her. This is called keeping yourself company for hours.

"Don't you get bored running alone for that long?" the non-ultramarathoners ask.

Nope. I keep myself entertained with them imagined lady folks.

Running alone is what you see. Having fantastic and flirtatious conversations is what actually happens during those long runs. There are the monumental conversations with my therapist while we trot along, and there are the in-depth discussions about sex my current crush and I delve into. I've had extensive exchanges with women I admire—women who don't even know I exist. It's fun. Makes me feel special. Thus, the solitary body keeping in motion helps to let the soul have some head space in order to be happy—to give my imagination the space it needs to wander.

Other questions asked when I tell people I run ultramarathons:

- What's that?
- Why?
- You run fifty miles *all at once*?
- Do you sleep?
- Do you eat?
- Are you crazy?

The best response I ever got when I told someone I ran fifty-mile races:

- You must really enjoy running.

Yup. Sure do. Because it's about getting the body moving, getting it out into an alone space which then bestows the space to expand.

Angie was never a woman I conversed with during my runs, because I have a desire for adventure, not that certain brand of bland, forced, so-so satisfaction.

Angie did, at one point, put forth into the world a single fantasy when we tried to do something about our floundering sex life.

A real-life example of lesbian bed death: Two women flirt, they fall in love, then have a bunch of sex, then get bored with each other, then avoid each other, then stop getting along, then say bye-bye to sex. And so, Sunday morning long runs were necessary in order to actually *feel* my body, to get out of the restricted head space my mind always found itself in after being around Angie for more than a half-hour.

The fantasy she put forth:

"Maybe I'll surprise you one morning," she teased, by which I mean put a smirk on her face and a belittling bitch in her throat. "You'll be finishing up your run, and I'll jump out from behind a tree. Then I'll push you up against that tree, and take your clothes off, and make love to you right there." Well, okay then. While the fantasy was pretty good, her delivery of its lines were a monotonic mess. A dull fantasy voice? Boring. Unsurprisingly, this tree incident never occurred.

What did happen, however, is that we did have good sex once. After a twenty-eight mile run, during which my body accumulated enough free space to pack it up and take it home with me like a souvenir from a foreign place I couldn't wait to return to, my skin tingled with a satisfying sense of accomplishment. In order to address that skin-tingling sense, I asked for sex. I can't remember if I had an orgasm that day or not. I'm not quite sure that's relevant here. Guessing games lead you nowhere.

Right now, my body feels wasted, spent. Dead legs. Eight hours of lactic acid building up in hamstrings and quadriceps and whatever the shin muscles are called (muscles of the shin nether regions, perhaps). (Do shin muscles even have a name?) Plus, two black toenails popped off around mile thirty-five and forty-six, along with the scratches on my palms and knees from falling after tripping on a tree root—the action of which popped that aforementioned second toenail right off—all make my body feel a bit like lead. A lot like lead, actually. And concrete, too. I could metaphor the shit out of my energy-depleted, dead-feeling body all day, because I can't move, so what the hell else do I have to do? It's seven hours after I stopped my stopwatch at the finish line (fifty miles in 8:02:05 bitches!) and moving my body is simply an absurd notion. Standing? Well, that's a bit incomprehensible right now. Climbing stairs? BWAHAHAHA. Fuck that.

But there's another feeling swelling up in my body. That vibrating sense of "Hell yeah I just ran fifty miles!" Where my spirit feels a bit floaty in my blood, and there's also this tingling sensation prancing around my skin. Especially the clit skin. My two vag lips pulsating all over the place. The labia bits of my lady parts swishing and swaying with each other for every step during those eight hours is why I'll be feeling a little orgasm-ish for the next few days.

It's about time.

What do you mean by that, Chelsey?

Let me put things in perspective here: I feel more sex-tingling desire rise in me after eight hours of running than the cumulative amount of sex-craving I ever felt for Angie in those four years of *us*. What a shame. Such a waste. So now I run fifty miles, chasing down my desire.

In Colorado, I walked **through** the forest alone.

1. When Angie and I fought about the amount of time I spent running, I got through those hours knowing I would go on a long run the next morning—for no other reason than to piss her off.

2. There was a moment when I thought, "I *do* love Angie. We can make it through this wretchedness." And then I laughed, because I knew that was so *not* true. Angie poked her nose up from behind Nietzsche and asked what was so funny.

3. Angie insisted on getting cats. I wanted my dog. She wanted cats. I lost my dog. She got her cats. I

forfeited so we could stop fighting about it. As I had feared, Angie never cleaned up after the cats. Fishing out cat shit from the litter box one day, I found myself sifting through the hard stuff we thought was a part of love. I found nothing but old bullshit that needed to be thrown out. No reason to keep what sinks.

4. Angie and I once sat through a performative lecture that shed light on our relationship. I jotted down a quote from the final act: "Do not fuck anyone you wouldn't want to be. Do not be anyone you wouldn't want to fuck." I never wanted to be a philosopher, as I found it restricted my imagination too much. Angie loved philosophy, would get her PhD in it, become a certified, structured thinker. According to the quote, I should have left, *now*.

5. Three years later, I finally did admit it. "I am through with you."

In Colorado, I walked through the forest alone.

But about the forest.

In the forest next to my house in Elizabeth, I found a bowling pin and chunks of AstroTurf. I somehow figured that the forest used to be a campsite, or maybe an RV park. Made sense to my seven-year-old mind. My suspicions were confirmed when I discovered the rusted metal signs with numbers painted on them hanging from different trees—marking some past parking spaces, perhaps? But there were no roads or trails leading up to these ideas of parking spaces. Just signs, and the random metal fencepost connected to no fence. And yet I stuck with the RV hypothesis, as it also somehow explained the bowling pin I found sticking up from the dirt. Because bowling pins are naturally found in RV parks, right? Astroturf, too. Of course. This reasoning proves the fact that, when given enough physical space and freedom, I have quite the imagination.

Between my house and the forest was a road that was more like a trail. It led to an imaginary tree house. This tree house probably belonged to the boy who lived in my house before me, but I'm not quite sure a boy lived in my house before me. I say it was imaginary, because there was one plank of wood nestled in the Y of the thick tree trunk, and nothing more. One piece of plywood not even nailed down to the tree; it was just shoved up there. This tree porch had no walls, no roof, no looking-out point for the dangers of the world. Just a plank of wood, a spot that provided a great view of the mountains and the valleys leading up to them, a space that allowed my mind to wander.

Well hello, theme.

The plank that was not a tree house sat watch over my real house, as my real house sat watch over my favorite forest.

Maybe my love for this forest grew from its strangeness. Instead of chilling indoors and talking on the phone, like my older sister did, I meandered alone through the endless possibilities of that forest. The oddities I found would help to release my imagination. I would poke around trees, tall weeds, yucca plants, and bushes. The Smurf Forest. I would get lost in the maze of my own made-up stories—became addicted to that feeling, actually.

If one were to tally up the number of things I'm addicted to, the list would be that of every noun in existence. You got something for me? I don't care what the hell it is. I want more.

More running, because at one point a hobby turned into a habit, then an identity and a necessity. Though, I do take pride in my running. And before I became a whacked-out drunk, I took pride in the amount of liquor I could glug on my own.

Addiction is all about pride. It's about showing off, in a way.

Though there is one addiction I had that embarrasses me. The concept of getting pulled in, or perhaps it's more like sucked in, that I shame myself for is my addiction to Angie. Yes, it's true. While I didn't necessarily like the woman, I was drawn in by her red hair and couldn't break away from the emotionally abusive bond we eventually created with each other.

Yes, I was addicted to her for a little while. The first six months or so. What else is there to do except fuck from the fascination of what a new body feels like rubbing up against my flesh? Regardless if I wanted to or not, whether it was healthy or not, I couldn't stop thinking about her in that blissful honeymoon stage that then quickly fizzled out.

And yet I stayed.

I stayed, because seven months into the relationship, the addiction of not wanting to deal with a dumb relationship settled in, took over our interactions. Silenced me.

Sssshhhhhhhhhhhhhhhhh? You hear that? It's the truth speaking. And this is what it says: *What the fuck was I thinking?*

In Colorado, I walked through the forest **alone**.

It's been twenty-one years since my forest walks. I'm in that wonderful post-Angie place in my life, and I realize I don't need those fifty miles to get some headspace—just a good twenty or so once a week to keep me smiling, sane. The four-year Angie hootenanny ended in a bad break-up that involved a lot of screaming and sobbing on her part, and packing a duffle bag of clothes and books on my part. I'm relieved to say that I have fully recovered from the trauma of dating Angie and now have all the mental meadows I need to attend to my thoughts about other women. Women I admire. Women who I would want to be—women I would not only want to fuck, but would also want to share my head space with. Like the you I thought of while I was running my fifty-mile race earlier this afternoon in Wisconsin.

It's night now, and my sore body needs to rest, be caressed. So I bring back into my mind my images and imagined conversations of the you I ran with for fifty miles today. The invisible relationship continues: You are lying in my bed next to me during a time in which the beginning of something might evolve into a you-and-me sort of thing. You ask me to tell you a story, because you, like me, are having a hard time going to sleep. My legs hurt. You're just a bad sleeper. So I mull over which story to tell you, because I want it to feel good on your skin. I want to skip the sad parts, but also not get too funny with it, because, after all, we are trying to get to sleep.

It is the story about the forest in Colorado I used to walk through alone at seven. Holding the pillow I know is too small to be your body—and that doesn't faze me at all because it *could* feel like a part of you, so I'll go with that, and besides the color of the pillowcase is similar to the darker ring of brown that circles your pupils before jumping into the black—I begin to rock you to sleep with words about space and nature and childhood independence and imagination and wandering and discovering. There is the road that was more like a trail. The rickety swing set with butt-piercing splinters. The seven acres of yucca plants surrounding my house. The prancing deer. And in all of these details about trees and yards and bowling pins and mountains and imagined tree houses, my mind suddenly recalls how the neighbors at the end of our long gravel driveway raised peacocks.

And so now I'm fully awake and am trying to figure out the veracity of that story. You—the you who doesn't even know you're here—listen about my forest and the possible peacocks. This peacock detail throws me off, because here I was telling you, who's really a pillow, about my childhood, and now there's this brilliantly colored exotic bird sitting in the middle of it, and it all feels so fantastical. As if it's too much to be real, because now, in my made-up conversations with the you who's not really here, I'm concerned with telling the facts. I need to know if these birds were really there or not. I want to text my mom and ask her if our neighbors in Elizabeth did, indeed, raise peacocks. But it's late, and what if my mother answers with *What the hell are you talking about?* How would that fit into my story for you? The story was supposed to be comfortable and soothing, something about how physical freedom can create a calm and open mind, but now there's this bizarre story about exotic animals that just shouldn't exist in small town Colorado. Birds that might have been a part of my imagination as I wandered through that free space of the forest.

Another random detail: the bowling pin in the middle of my forest. So the sensible lullaby was shot to hell long before the peacock.

This story keeps us awake and giggling, and I kiss the soft pillow that is not the top of your head, and realize. For a second, the brown pillow and one-way giggles feel more real and plausible than a peacock. But in my head, I'm pretty damn sure the peacock was there. I know for a fact that you are not here.

I am alone.

In my head.

There is space.

I've known it since I was seven.

In Colorado, I walked through the forest alone.

The Family Jewels

In July of 1999, I ate out my first pussy. In March 2012, I blow-jobbed a man for the first time, the event of which reminded me of my grandmother.

Let me explain.

June 2011, my grandmother is talking with her two daughters (my aunt and my mother) and she whispers:

"Did you know that women put men's penises in their mouths, *and* there's a word for it?!?"

What my mother says later on when she relates this story to me:

"Guess my father never got a blow job."

Due to my lesbianism, I have only slept with/blow-jobbed one man in my life—the man who became my husband who made me a hasbian—and so aside from my own recent personal experiences fellating a certain fellow, the only other tale I have about blow jobs is the one about my grandmother's naivety on the subject.

Thanks for the story, granny.

Wait, I lie. I do have another story!

2004, a quote from my mother: "Your three-year-old nephew looks like he's giving a blow job."

My mother said this because she gave Dylan a squishy, peach-colored plastic octopus to play with and he kept putting the long head of it in his mouth. I actually suspect my nephew will grow up to be gay. Not because of this incident, but because even though I am a lesbian who is now married to a man, I still have excellent gaydar.

But I was talking about my grandmother.

My grandmother has slapped my ex-girlfriend's ass. My grandmother has slapped my best friend's ass. She has slapped my sister's girlfriend's ass. All three of these slappees are actually one person. That would be Sabrina.

Sabrina is my ex-girlfriend turned best friend turned my sister's girlfriend.

Back in 2002, I was just 19 and crying in my grandmother's guest bedroom about how my girlfriend cheated on me. "I don't understand the whole lesbian thing," my grandmother said. And then she followed with the statement, "but I love you anyway." She had come into the room to console me, but initially her presence just made me feel awkward, as I didn't want to talk about my lesbian life with my seventy-ish-year-old grandmother. And then she said that statement, how she loved me anyway, and the honesty and sweet-old-lady-ness of it gave me comfort, consoled me.

A decade later my grandmother still loves me anyway, though she's probably a tad bit confused about my sexuality as she attends a wedding in which her lesbian granddaughter (me) marries a man. And soon she will love my sister anyway, because on the night that this hasbian (me) marries a dude, my married heterosexual sister does her own little sexuality shuffle and hooks up with my best friend/ex-girlfriend, Sabrina. My sister was able to do this act of hooking up because I told her that her asshole husband—who I hated dearly—was not allowed to come to my wedding. My sister was fine with this, because she didn't like him, either. It had something to do with him strangling her a few times. So without her husband in tow, my sister found herself momentarily liberated from the socially-constructed standardized-sexuality expectations she has always followed for her entire life, the ones that tell her that, because she is a woman, she can only date men. At the wedding, though, she was finally free—if only for a weekend—to be whatever she wanted to be and to do whatever she wanted to do. With this brief opportunity of freedom, she decided to kiss a girl for the first time. And she liked it.

A year after my grandmother stated that she didn't understand lesbianism but loved me anyway, she met my best friend, Sabrina, who was by then my ex-girlfriend from a long time ago (like 12 years long) because we dated for two weeks in high school but broke up because we couldn't stand the way each other kissed. And when my grandmother met Sabrina, she patted her ass as she hugged her hello, her old wrinkly hands getting some young, lesbian ass action. This ass-tapping characteristic trait of my now eighty-eight year old grandmother is something I can always count on to happen. It's just her way of saying *welcome*.

It is now 2013, and when my grandmother pats Sabrina's ass, now she is tapping that ass of my sister's girlfriend, because now, at thirty-three years of age, my sister is gay with my best friend.

My grandmother has yet to realize this, and no one in the family will tell her, because we figure that she will just figure it out on her own when she's ready to figure it out. And who knows if she ever will, but you would think it would be obvious, considering my sister is now separated from her husband and lives with her three kids in the same house as the known-dyke Sabrina, *and* Sabrina and her share a bed *and* the kids call Sabrina "Mama #2."

Fucking cute, huh?

For the entirety of my life, my grandmother and grandfather never shared a bed. I'm sure they did when they were younger, what with the proof of two daughters and all, but as they aged, their old and withering bodies retreated to not only their own beds each night, but their own bedrooms, as well. Perhaps, when you've been married for sixty years, a good night's sleep is better than cuddling with the other pea in your pod.

My grandfather died last year. He had a stroke and was in hospice for three weeks before he kicked it. There, he lost some of the functioning in his brain that helped him to stand and walk. Because of this, he wasn't able to get out of the hospital bed in order to go to the bathroom. This fact resulted in him frequently peeing in his bed. My aunt and mother were there to help the nurses wipe him clean and to change the bedding. And while participating in this messy yet necessary duty, for the first time in her life my mother observed the size of her father's penis, on which she later commented:

"My mother must have been very sexually satisfied her whole life."

And while at that point in my life I hadn't slept with a man yet, when I helped to change my grandfather's bedding later on that night, I could see what my mother was talking about. In 2011, at the age of twenty-eight, my grandfather's penis became the first one I saw in real life. And, compared to the dildos I have briefly seen before they went inside of me—most of which were some whacky color and unrealistically long—I believed my mother's statement to be true.

I say my grandfather's penis was the first one I saw in "real life" because, up to that point, I had only ever laid my eyes on representations of the male genitalia twice:

1. Random porn watching
2. Looking at pictures of my aunt.

Again, let me explain.

July 2009, I saw a picture of the Biggest. Cock. Ever. It was my aunt's cock. Her workplace was having a costume party, and being the outrageously funny co-worker that she is, my aunt decided to dress up like something that necessitated covering her whole body with a cloth contraption that resembled a huge penis. The shaft tipped above her head and the testicles swept along the floor near her feet. In addition to the cock part of her costume, she also had a long peacock feather attached to the backside of the pale pink costume as if it were a tail. And because the big penis around her body was distracting everyone from seeing the peacock feather on her ass, she had to point out this imperative portion of her costume so that everyone would understand what she was dressed as. A cocktail. In 2009, I went out for cocktails with my aunt and she showed me a picture of the costume. And yes. She was a cock—a cock with a tail.

This was three years before I slept with a man for the first time. And when I first engaged in heterosexual behaviors (WTF?!?) in March 2012, we were on my bed fully clothed and highly aroused, and I told him to "show me the goods." He did just that, and I stared for a bit at the penis pointing at me, feeling lucky that I was the chosen one to whom that penis decided to point. It reminded me of the Spin-the-Bottle games in middle school in which I prayed that during my turn the bottle would stop spinning on one of the women, any of the women, really, in the circle. This happened a few times, making me feel like a lucky little lesbian-to-be even though we just exchanged pecks on the cheeks. And now it is twelve years after those lovely girly spin-the-bottle cheek-pecks, and there is a penis pointing at me, singling me out from the lesbians of the world as I become an official hasbian.

I do not know if my grandmother will ever understand bisexuality, but I do know she will love me anyway. I know this just like I knew she would tap my husband's ass when they first met. Which is exactly what she did, her old wrinkly hands getting some young man ass action. Lately, there has been an increase of cougars in society—not the animal, but the older women who flirt with and sleep with younger men. And while my grandmother is now aware of blow-jobbing, I am in no way worried about her cougaring my husband. She just isn't that kind of older lady. Instead, my grandmother gets quite a lot of satisfaction from some good ol' ass-slapping the thin skin of her translucent palms getting a good handful of young, plump flesh. I say rock it while you can, granny. Live it up before you croak.

The Guide to Kissing Like a Butterfly

When I think of eyelashes, I think of kisses. Kid me kissing my mid-30's mom, specifically. Butterfly kisses. Our lashes lightly flapping fluttering flickering tickling each other's smooth-skinned cheeks, each eyelash's tender touch a *goodnight* and an *I love you* and a *sleep tight* susurrating on the soft facial surfaces of this mother-daughter pair. It's around 9pm or whatever time a nine-year-old's bedtime is, and mom's tucking me tightly into my lower bunk. The top one is occupied. Not by my sister. She's across the hall whispering to some girl on the phone about some boy. The space of my top bunk has been hijacked by a mountain range of stuffed animals I force myself to have an affinity for, because that's how nine-year-old girls function in the world—holding onto and hugging wads of cotton squished into the shape of an animal, contained by some synthetic material doing a poor imitation of an actual animal—an animal that you, in fact, would most likely never hold nor hug were you to come across a real version of it. Such as a bear.

Last week, I convinced my grandmother to buy me a beat-up Snoopy-looking stuffed animal at the Goodwill, because I wanted to feel attached to something. The Snoopy doppelganger looked like how a nine-year-old's favorite stuffed animal should look. Like a battered spouse. Like something you love to death.

In truth, I didn't give a flying nothing about stuffed anythings, though that sentiment made me feel guilty and abnormal. So I hung onto whatever stuffed animals were bestowed upon me for every holiday, of which there were many because my family knew I had a top bunk full of stuffed things and so they wanted to add to the collection in order to contribute to the core of my identity which was supposedly comprised of being a stuffed animal lovin' nine-year-old girl. But the horses and rabbits and sheep and ring-tailed monkey (yes, really) never meant anything to me except for the fact that I felt weird and/or left out for being a nine-year-old girl with an aversion to anything that could be described as *plush*. And so, I faked it. I held them and hugged them and kissed their foreheads when in the presence of family. I piled them on my top bunk as if I wanted—no, wait, scratch that—as if I *needed* them, because by god I would have just died if they didn't "sleep" on the bunk above me, protecting me from all of the evil in the world that could potentially come kill me at night. Such as a bear.

When I think about kisses, I think back to when my mother's flapping flickering tickling eyelashes fluttered along my cheek as we kissed each other goodnight, emulating butterflies. But soon my reminisces are usurped by the memory of the supposedly cute stuffed creatures assembling and then eventually amalgamating into a pastel mountain range of *plush* on the bunk above me. The pile was a blur of pale pink, pale blue, pale purple, pale yellow and every other color whose hue is seriously lacking strong chromatic content (an art term which is often referred to by the much simpler term "desaturated," (or, for the extremely color-naming illiterate folks like me, "soft," which, fittingly in this context, can be a synonym for "plush")). The amassed jumble of soft and unmoving residents commandeering the apex of my double-decker bed, which is to say the stuffed animals up top, only exist in my adult mind as a swirl of washed-out color. Due to previous reasons as detailed above (re: my disliking of stuffed, plushy shit), and since I kept them out of my sight by throwing them on the top bunk that was taller than me and thus I couldn't see them unless I climbed the ladder in an effort to look at them, which I never did because I didn't like them—by now, dear reader, this should not be a big shocker—the size of my memory in regards to the specifics of the lurking stuffed animals is about as thick as an eyelash.

Though a few stand out. Such as the bear. That big brown one that to this day I still do not know if it was actually supposed to be some type of bear sitting like bears sit with their asses on the ground. (I have never actually seen a real bear, let alone one sitting on its ass with its back legs splayed out in front of it, but I say these things as if I do know them, because when you're nine you know things such as how bears sit, because, duh, of course that's what they do. Everyone knows that. Just look at all the bear stuffed animals—they're all sitting like that.)

If it was not a bear, then the big, brown, plush animal-like shaped thing could have been a fat, wrinkled dog sitting on its ass as if it was a bear. A pug, giant with gargantuan wrinkles of sorts. Due to the quadruple Mount Everest mountain range of wrinkles that added some serious elevation to its facial topography, the bear-impersonating pug's eyes were completely hidden.

The enlarged pug sitting bear-style had a rip in its chest. Plastic nylon like fishing line that possibly was fishing line had pulled away from the animal of an indeterminate origin's chest, unstitching itself. Plumes of cotton burst from the chest wound. I was completely enamored with taking two fingers and pushing said escapee cotton back into the chest-wounded brown animal while pretending I was actually jabbing at its heart.

Pluto was probably on the top bunk, too. It was a huge stuffed animal of that stupid Disney character I found annoying. And so why did I own it, one must wonder? Explanation: I was six years old and at Disney World with my family when my dad got a horrible headache and left his "girls" (aka wife and two daughters) in the gift shop with his credit card and told us to get whatever we wanted as he had to retreat to the hotel room to attend to the killer pain.

(I don't actually remember any of this. The past sentence is brought to you by mom telling me stories. Reliable narrator? Meh. Re-commence translation of mom's memory.)

My dad had said *whatever I wanted* and so I did the most sensible and obvious thing one should do when told "get whatever you want." I got the biggest stuffed animal in that gift shop.

His fault. He said *a-n-y-t-h-i-n-g*.

And so I said "Pluto!" as if the rest of my life's happiness depended on my possession of that one stuffed animal.

For those who have not been counting, let's check in and take inventory of the stuffed animals we have thus far. There are three to tick off on our role call.

1) Domestic violence survivor Snoopy

2) Obese pug sitting bear-style

3) The largest stuffed animal Disney World sold in their gift shop circa 1989

One other cotton-stuffed character that was possibly stationed on my bed's observation deck was a life-sized doll from when I was three, whom I named April (my birthday month). Each appendage was its own cylindrically-shaped piece of cloth stuffed with a wad of cotton. In compliance with proper appendage placement, the arms and legs were sewn onto the rightful shoulders and hips with loosely-tied cotton twine, which allowed all of the appendages to play helicopter. The head sector of this stuffed doll had April's face sewn onto it. I believe her eyes were buttons. To recap: windmill appendages and a fixed button glare and all of it was life-sized. File her under *shit that creeped me out* and cross-reference that with *shit that still creeps me out*. My great-grandmother made her. My great-grandmother died within a few days of gifting her to me. (And the file containing the creepies thickens.)

Also riding overhead was a red Valentine's Day teddy bear with a white stomach and "Love me" tatted onto its abdomen courtesy of the invention of embroidery.

One, maybe two, of these stuffed things had eyelashes. I can't remember exactly which ones. Though my bet's on April and tatted up V-day bear. Pluto was the dude version, so no girl-determining eyelashes there. Pugbear Minotaur had those folds of "skin," so you couldn't even see its eyes, let alone discern if there were fake eyelashes adorning them. (I am actively resisting, and now failing to resist, making a comment here about where the bear was probably made—in China where most teddy bear-bearing wombs are located, and how it wouldn't surprise me to learn that the child workers who never got to hold, hug nor squeeze the stuffed animals they made (see file labeled: *wages, shit*) were instructed by America to sew in eyelashes with their foreign, nimble fingers even though one couldn't see Pugbear Minotaur's eyes, because goddamn it America needed to be able to discern which ones were the girls!)

It's 9:05pm and I'm still a nine-year old girl lying in bed—albeit five minutes older than I was five minutes ago—thinking about eyelashes. I'm all tucked in with the proof that I'm trying to "fit in" loitering, hovering above my head. But none of that matters, now, because I'm falling asleep with a sense of safety that has never been and never will be brought on by holding onto and/or hugging an object that can be described with the adjective *plush*, but instead can only be induced by the feel of my mother's eyelashes flapping fluttering flickering tickling my cheek. Butterfly kisses.

What You Finally Attend To

You are fully aware of the fact that you are a lesbian. You are fully aware of the fact that he is a straight man. And you are fully aware of the fact that your underwear is sopping wet right now because you are thinking about him. This has been going on for nine years.

But during those nine years, you were a lesbian and he was a straight man and you had a crush on him but there was that whole lesbian/straight man dynamic thing going on, so what could you do? You shrugged your shoulders. And yet your body and your wants persisted. The fantasies you couldn't fight. How they pressed on your skin, surged through your blood, unable for you to ignore.

Nine years go by.

And then it is February, 2012, and the two of you start up a conversation about erotica on Facebook. Thank you, social media website.

The two of you talk.

By the end of that seven-hour long talk, you, the lesbian, have told him about the crush you have always had on him, and he, the straight dude, has told you about the crush he has always had on you, and you have chatted about fucking each other and you have taken a few masturbating breaks and by the end of it all he has purchased bus tickets and in two weeks will take a 26-hour bus ride to come see you.

He takes a 26-hour bus ride to come see you.

And then he comes.

And then you come.

And then he raises up his head and he says, *God I love eating pussy!*

And then you say, *Me too!*

And then you, the lesbian, are dating a man.

And as you date this man, you are fully aware of yourself, of how you have finally attended to your sopping wet underwear.

You inform your mother of this radical shift in your sexuality. She is a bit shocked. She has always liked your girlfriends, always accepted you for who you are. And so this time around, when there is another flip in your sexuality, she's the one who says, "It doesn't matter what gender the other person is as long as you love them," which is the exact same thing you said to her twelve years ago when you first declared yourself a lesbian.

You as a lesbian: the girlfriends, the gay bars, the one night stands with softball dykes, the crushes on coaches, the picking of pubes from teeth, the way you drool at women who smoke cigarettes. Twelve years of picking pubes. Twelve years of drooling. Yes. Lesbian.

But now there is a man inside you. A man who is your best friend, who is your only male friend, who is the only man you would ever let slip himself inside of you. This, in a way, is what you have been waiting for. The dildos did a fantastic job, but there was always that nagging feeling of wanting something more.

Perhaps it was that something about him that nagged at you for that something more.

Funny story: You wouldn't have met him had it not been for your lesbianism. You were a senior in high school and didn't know where to go to college, so you asked your boss, who you had a crush on, what to do. She told you to apply to her alma mater. You loved her so much, wanted her so much, that you would do anything to make her happy, to make her approve of you, and hopefully like you and perhaps have sex with you, so of course you didn't say no. You applied. You applied to a college you knew nothing about. You were fully aware of the fact that the only reason why you applied to this college is that you had a slim hope that maybe your crush/boss would visit you once a year during homecoming. To you, that once a year was reason enough. She wrote the letter of recommendation. You went to the interview in which you were asked odd questions you didn't understand the purpose of—such as, Which three things would you bring with you to college in order to remember your past? Picture. Journal. What-the-fuck-ever.

You got in.

And it was at that college from which your crush had just graduated, the crush who led you there, that you met him. Instantly, he slips into your mind. Penetrates your thoughts. You don't know how or why, but he does. You resist being fully aware of this. You are most certain you are a lesbian. You have a gay pride tattoo. So there is no hope here. Even when he is your roommate for two years and you actively have to resist kissing him goodnight. Even when you have dreams about him that make your underwear sopping wet. Even then, there's the fact of a forever-a-lesbian with a big gay rainbow on your ankle going on. So yes, no hope here.

And yet.

The hope holds out for nine years. And then you have that Facebook conversation in which you type in those specific "I have a crush on you" confessional words, and then he dittos them, and then he takes a 26-hour bus ride to come see you, and then he slips himself inside you, and then you transition from being a lesbian to being a hasbian, and then five months later you are married to him. And you will stand on the wrong sides of each other during the ceremony because you are breaking tradition (and there will be no white dress but a cherry red cocktail dress and silver sparkling high heels and there will be no march down the aisle but a two-step down it with your mother), and your lesbian friends will be there to woot you on.

Yes. You are fully aware of the irony, of how if it weren't for your lesbianism, your crush on another woman, you would not have gone to that college, would not have met him, would not have felt this pleasure, this remedy to the sopping wet underwear, would not have finally admitted that you wanted to commit yourself to him for, well, forever.

So you are fully aware of the fact that the lesbians helped to deliver him to you.

And to that you slip off your sopping wet underwear, straddle the man you never thought you would allow yourself to straddle, and you say thank you, lesbians, thank you.

Curtains

When we got to the lake house, I broke the curtains and you cried. It wasn't that I bent the rod or ripped bits of thick maroon fabric that made the tears flow from your eyes. No, it was that you were going through a divorce. This fact had nothing to do with the curtains, but they were curtains in this house, the one you and your husband used to visit. The maroon curtains were stitched with bits of gold, and the bed I slept in was red velvet. It was the bed you and he used to sleep in when you visited this lake house. You wouldn't come into my room. It was too hard. The memory of him tucked too tightly inside it. I tried to trick you one night to walk in there. You were across the hall in the bathroom brushing your teeth. *Hey Ally!* I called from the red velvet bed. *Come here.* You walked over to the room, hung your body in the doorway. *No. Come here.* I motioned you towards the bed. You took a step forward, one toe entering the room swollen with him, then froze. I smiled. *You got one step in.* You said you couldn't do it. You just couldn't do it. But you smiled at me anyway.

This was four nights after I broke the curtains, and a few days since I fixed them. Nothing was really broken, just a little bent out of shape. The rod straightened out easily enough, the rips unseen once I re-hung the curtain. Nothing unfixable. But not so with your marriage. Not with the man who was a decade full of lies, the husband fraught with a sex addiction. The pedophilia he never told you about. This broke you. And the marriage crumbled. Irreparable.

We were at your family's lake house in northern Minnesota on a writing retreat. You, the famous author, had brought me, the writer who couldn't figure out how to express herself. The lake sat outside the screened-in porch, the porch we camped out in with our cigarettes and our laptops and the large silver bowl brimming with black cherries. You finished a book proposal, then started writing poetry. A poem about time's arrow came out of that trip, about how chaos erupts because one event leads to another. You were thinking about him. I wrote an essay about grief and sobbed on the grass outside the porch, sitting under a tree, squashing the ants that surrounded me, unwittingly.

This was the week my grandfather was dying.

One night towards the end of the trip, I held onto your thumb. I was still deciding what you meant to me, if I loved you more than a friend should love a friend. When I curled up behind your back because I was sad, when you tucked your little paw-like feet underneath my own, and when your thumb curled around and caressed my thumb, I knew I was in love with something different. In love with a friend, a deep kind of love only friends can know. I slept beside you, but not really. I closed my eyes, pretending to sleep, feeling your own grief sink into the mattress of the yellow foldaway couch. You chose the couch over the room with too many memories. I chose that night to curl into you, allowing our friendship to hold my grief.

Chelsey Clammer

The next night I fell asleep on the floor beside your bed reading a book of essays. You, on your foldaway mattress, had also fallen asleep with a book between your hands. Poetry drifting your eyes closed, caressing your skin asleep. I woke up knowing the fireworks were about to burst, that another year of America had turned, that we had to celebrate it by ripping open the sky. Brilliant reds and yellows reflected off the lake. You slept through them, slept heavily in your sinking boat of grief. Later, I watched the sky rupture with lightning, heard the fracture of thunder, nature's white crackling overpowering America's celebration. I saw the bright colors recede, surrender, give way to the white streaks. I thought about what must die. My grandfather. Love. And then the erupting sky tired, tucked itself in, slept, expired.

BodyHome

4 a.m. is my favorite color. It's when the quiet, dark sky cuddles with the air, when a crepuscular shade full of stillness and possibility inhabits the world. The morning hours swell with dreams. As I wake up to them my body unfurls, opens to the solace.

My feet thump on the ground, extract my body from the me-shaped dent in the soft mattress, cross my room in six steps, and tuck myself behind my desk. I light two candles and gaze into their glow. The flame, my brain yawns open. My notebook sits in front of me, the last words I wrote from the night before stare up, want more. *How do we listen to desire?* A question not begging for an answer, but wants more questioning, more consideration. There is blank space waiting to be filled; I tuck my dreadlocks behind my ear and pick up my blue pen.

Up until this point, the point where my body is positioned above my words and ready to make more, my bed has been desired most. Not out of tiredness, but to get back into that space at the end of each day in which I am a body being, a body still with itself, a body dreaming. I sit at my black desk, stare past the shushing candlelight, and my eyes linger on the sight of my bed, the dark green quilt crumpled to one side, the brown top sheet urging

175

me to come back. This is not about sleeping, but dreaming. Desiring that space in which my body is mine, my home. The home I curl into at night, the body I crawl into when the world exhales. The body that is a home I slip into, the quietly lying skin. It is skin I grasp in awe of its presence, persistence, elasticity, growth. And in the morning, in this morning as in every morning, the night's reveries of living fully in my body continue to drift around my head, hum along my skin.

Because this is my dream, my desire: to live. To live fully in this body, to make this body that space of safety, of home. It is one dream constantly in the making, one perpetually shifting its shape. There is growth in the world with each breath, each dream, each time I lay down to sleep, to settle into my skin. And so I seek sleep, seek the space of myself with my desires, my bodyhome.

SLEEPING

Eight years old and lying in the back seat of my mom's car. She drives my sister and me home from swim practice, guides us through the dark, the world full of stars, and aims us toward our beds. I close my eyes and pretend to sleep. This is really escaping into the desires of my mind, the dreams that are in my body, the ones that feel safe and cozy. I keep my eyes closed, feel around inside my head, dream of my body as it becomes a body being hugged, skin being loved by women, women I am starting to become attracted to. In the car, the bump between the two bucket seats curves up into my ribs, prevents me from finding a comfortable position. But I'm snug in my mind, finally having sunk into the space where I dream of womanly arms embracing me tightly. Smile. Continue to keep my eyes closed to the world that tells me not to want this, these woman hugs. But in the dark, with my eyes closed, I am safe at home in these dreams, settle into my tired body that slips into the desires of my mind.

These are fantasies of love, of feeling safe and well-held. These are older women from whom I seek comfort, an enveloping embrace. My second grade teacher, strong female characters from TV. Murphy Brown, Angela in *Who's the Boss*. Women who are old enough to be my mom, who could give me big, motherly hugs. Dreams of soft skin against my own, of falling asleep in a woman's arms that hold me steady, keep my growing body together.

My eyes are closed to the back of my mom's seat. I tune out the conversations she has with my older sister and concentrate on this idea of a hug. My mom navigates the car home, and my body tingles with each curve through the forests of Colorado as we speed closer to home, to my bunk bed, to my room swathed in posters of strong female characters from TV.

When we reach the house, I curl into my mattress, hug my arms against my budding chest, settle into my resting place where dreams blossom in my body. In my bed, the feeling of comfort and safety stretches, grows.

Chelsey Clammer

BODY TAKING

I am twenty years old and wake up to a lover's hands. Her fingers grasp my shoulders, her legs straddle my naked stomach. I had been waiting for her return, for her to come home from the bar and curl into her arms, fall asleep. But I fell into sleep on my own. And now here she is, disrupting dreams. She has crashed into the bed, stumbled onto my body. She has fumbled the comforter away from my skin, and now on top of me, she pries open my arms, the naked skin of my belly. Her alcohol-drenched breath.

There is her silhouette. The room a startling dark, except for the slant of hallway light flaring into her bedroom. The white light darkens her body, the negative space is unwanted. I was fine, alone, content in the dreams I can no longer remember.

Her body breathes fumes of whiskey onto my flesh. I try to slink away, to crawl further into skin from this, from what will come next.

Chelsey, come on, she slurs onto my exposed nipple.

The cocoon of my arms has been broken. She slithers down my body. There is no "no," because I do not know how. Because how do you say no to the lover whom you have said yes to for years?

She pries my legs apart; I rest my hands at my sides. My fingers are curled into fists as she twirls her own fingers around my pubic hair, parting it in order to dive in.

Closed eyes against her body and hallway light that spotlights this scene. Lids closed shut. Tears.

She sloppily licks away, pushes her fingers into places I no longer want to feel, and performs something she believes to be desire.

And then she passes out.

And then: roll over, cover my body with my hands; there is too much there to touch. I travel away from myself, lose the hold on my body that is no longer mine. There is now no desire to be enveloped—only grasping for the feeling of gone.

BODY BREAKING

It is night. I am twenty-five. My knees kneel inside of my closet near my bed. A plastic bag sits in front of me on the floor. In bright red letters, the side of the white bag tells me *Thank You Thank You Thank You* a dozen times. Thank you, it says. You're welcome, says my mess. My insides scream as I force them out of me, purging all of the food into the Thank You bag. The white plasticity holds the weight of what I couldn't resist to eat. Onion rings at the bar. Chips. Candy and cookies bought on the way home. I binged as I traveled. And at home, a loaf of bread with butter. Mashed potatoes. I consumed everything I could. Then, kneeling in the closet, toes grazing the bed, I took one of the bags acquired in the binging spree, and laid it out in front of me. On the wooden floor of my closet, I continue to dip my head into its Thank You messages.

And it all comes out. And in the closet with my hopes that the thin walls and wooden door will muffle the sound from my roommates, I continue to heave. My elbows and forearms circle the bag. The contents of my stomach come up easily with the alcohol that washed them down.

After I have brought up everything, after I have knotted the bag closed, sealed up the stench of my stomach, concealed the scent of my own embarrassment and pain, I drop the bag in my trashcan. Then, I wobble over to my dresser and grab my stashed bottle of whiskey. Popping the black, waxy cork off the Knob Creek and I take a swig. Cleansing my tongue of the vomit taste, the self-destruction continues. I then pick up a razor and begin to cut. It is the bulimia I want to cut out of my life. I slice reminders into my skin to not eat. Swipe. To be the socially-accepted anorexic instead of the disgusting buli-mic. Swipe. Each slice is a promise. Swipe. *I will not eat.* Swipe. *I will refuse food. Swipe.* The effects of these reminders seep out of my skin, soak into the t-shirt I have grabbed to wipe up the blood. A sight of red to remind me that this is what I want—to disappear, to gush away from myself. My disintegrating body is all I have to claim. And I don't want it.

I stumble into my bed with a swollen throat, blood soaked with alcohol, blood soaking through the shirt I wrapped around my arm. I smash into sleep with my thin skin wrapped tight around my bones. It is skin that triggers, skin that remembers the feeling of being perpe-tually raped by my ex-girlfriend. I continue to remove my body from myself, to let the notion of a body break away from my skin. Before I finally crash into the darkness of sleep, I vaguely wonder if I will wake up the next day. This is not sleeping; this is dying. I spill, splatter into a caesura from self-destruction. My nose drips. My blood drips. I dip further away from myself, ripped away from a body dreaming. This is a collection of fractured flesh, a heap of a body incapable of suturing itself into a sense of safety.

BODY SHIFTING

I wake up in the white-colored bed, the soft, pale comforter doing nothing to ease the pounding hangover in my head. Legs tangled in the fluff of white, ankles wrestling to free themselves from the heat, the down comforter presses into my skin, traps my alcohol-drenched blood underneath my covered flesh. I wrangle myself free from the covering, and throw my body over the edge of the bed. The mattress bends down, rejects my sweating skin from the comfort it doesn't give. It flings me out with disgust, tired of this body that constantly stinks and stains the serene white with alcohol, with drops of blood. I sway as I stand and reach down to the floor for the cloudy glass of vodka from the night before. I desperately chug at the last few drops fermenting in the bottom of the glass, my body brushing up against the bed as I lean over. But there is nothing left in the glass to quench this ugly feeling. Angry and irate, I stomp away from the bed, extract myself from the room that contains the mattress that gives no sleep, no dreams. My naked body bumps against the doorframe entering into the white hallway. If I can't drink my hang-over away, then I will binge and purge the sour feeling from my stomach. I travel the length of the swirling hall-way to the kitchen, and realize everything was binged and purged last night. With no food and no alcohol, I resort to the last thing that helps to steady my shaking hands.

I am suddenly standing in a bathroom. For now, this bathroom, that bed, are not places or things I own, but simply occupy. I was kicked out of my last roommate's apartment for binging on all of her food. The loaf of bread, the two boxes of noodles, her stash of cookies, everything I could ingest when drunk and out of my mind, again. She came home to an empty kitchen, her room-mate passed out down the hall. So she kicked me out and I found myself lost, broke, with nowhere to go.

Luckily, there are people in my life who love me more than I love myself. One of my bosses at work offered me this apartment. She owns a three bedroom, but is living at her girlfriend's house. Without asking for rent, without even asking if I wanted to move in, but more of demand-ing me to do it, she gave me her keys, expected me stay in her extra bed.

The bright white walls of the bathroom, the sun sting-ing my skin as it strikes the mirror through the window, these pierce my bloodshot eyes as I grab my razor that sits expectantly on the sink. I cut. I cut and something finally slashes into my brain. Finally. The cut changes something inside of me. Not just a feeling of pain or shame or something like momentary relief, but a cut that screams *This has to stop.* I look up at myself in the mirror.

My yellow and puffy skin stares back, waxy and bloated. My eyes are wobbly and full of red streaks, of burst blood vessels. I am repulsed by myself. I look away from this indication of a depressing and terrifying life, look down at the cut, and become even more disgusted. On my arm is evidence of my shameful life. The red seeps out, stares at me as I try not to gape at the gaping wound. I cannot look anymore, cannot continue to bear witness to this life.

With blood dripping down my arm, I go into the bedroom, the white bed glaring at me, pushing me to get out of there and do something about this urge to not do something horrible, again. I grab my phone. I call a friend, one of the three I have left in my life, one who did not retreat from me when I started to get scary. One who is not afraid to face my eating disorder, my alcoholism, my self-injury. I tell her what I know: If I stay home today, I'll continue to cut. And I won't stop until there is nothing left to cut.

We go to the ER. I sit slumpishly on the stiff hospital bed and answer a series of questions about suicide risk and self-injury. I tell them the truth, tell them that if they let me go home, I will cut again. They assess me, they agree, they know, they see it in my eyes, the desperation sitting—pleadingly—on my face. I sit on the hard hospital mattress, my legs swinging back and forth, swishing the white paper covering of the maroon mattress as I wait, as I yearn to move towards something else.

The heavy metal psych ward doors lead to a room dressed in depressing gray walls, and another uncomfortable hospital bed. This one is a blue plastic mattress that is

just a small bit of padding against the steel frame underneath. I curl my legs up to my chest and let out a sigh of
relief. In this stifling place, I will be taken care of, watched
over, forbidden to drink, to binge, to cut. And in this
uncomfortable bed, under the buzzing, florescent hospital lights, there are the beginnings of surrender, of finally
giving into the care.

BODY SOBERING

It is my second day in the hospital. There is a large dent
in the thin, plastic mattress, a mold of my body, of my
need to just lie and surrender myself. The door swings
open. A female social worker strides over to me, grabs my
stitched and scarred arm, and pulls me away from the
bed. My body unsuctions from the mattress. She takes my
hand as my legs creak with each step towards the
common room, towards my first AA meeting. I sit, gawk
at the other alcoholics. I do not want to be here. I am
stubborn, at first, do not want to admit to my problem of
alcohol even though I know it's the root, the initial action
that spurs all of my other problems. I just want to lie in
bed and soak and be nothing and not think about
anything but the mattress taking in my weight, sighing
with me. I am resistant to getting out of bed, to going to
AA, but go because I am there, because each day the
social worker comes and unsuctions me. Each day I
remove myself from the solace of my bed, temporarily
remove the heap of my body from the mattress to learn
about my problems. And after a few meetings, I start to

get it, start to see how I am powerless to alcohol and, hell yes, my life has become unmanageable.

I sit in a meeting on my ninth day in the hospital. I slump in a large, maroon-padded, wooden-framed chair, and there is a shift that takes place in my head. Something scoots its way into the space between my skin and my bones. There is a word that rattles my body: the syllables of *enough.* After the meeting finishes, I head back to the harsh florescent lights that beam down on my thin blue mattress that has become a place of solace. I lie down, my last night to lie down in the uncomfortable bed that has unexpectedly given me much relief. It is the bed in which I have started to caress my broken skin staring at the blue, cotton-weaved curtain. Scabs are flaking off, my body has sobered up, and my throat no longer tastes of blood. There is this feeling, this shift, this sense of *enough,* and I switch off the lights. I clasp my hands against my chest. I fall asleep, begin to dream.

BODY MAKING

It has been a month since the hospital, and while I am slowly stitching my life back together, forming a new way of living, the effects of abusive experiences, the destructive habits created from them, the ways in which I avoided my body for so long still linger.

I am on my way to work, getting on a train in Chicago. My commute has become a ritual of sitting in my body, mapping out the space she inhabits. Each day there are the obstacles of my mind as I judge the way my body moves. At the train stop, there is the turnstile, and it rushes up behind me as I push it with my hand. The metal bar hits the back of my overstuffed messenger bag that bustles with snacks for the day, with notes for my job. The metal hitting my bag does not indicate to me that I am carrying a large amount of stuff for work, but means I exist too much, take up too much space; there is too much of me in the world. Feeling the bar slap behind me, I intensely feel the curve of my butt and wish it wasn't there. Flat, barely visible, I would slip through unnoticed, untouched. But my body touches the metal every morning, and every morning I think my body is too much for the smallness I feel of it inside. I want to shirk away from my skin. My body touches the world, and it is too big. I hold onto this piece of judgment each day, this rubric for if I am or am not on the road to perfection, to still being able to slip a bit away, to that distorted place of a disappearing body that feels like safety. And while sober and safe, I still yearn to remove myself, to keep any side of me from touching the world. The game of Operation. To slip by untouched. When I do, no buzzers ring in my head.

This has to stop. I am growing weary of tiptoeing around myself, of not letting my feet fully hit the ground for fear of hearing myself live.

On the train, I keep my body rigid in the plastic seat so as not to touch the woman next to me. The brick city buildings slip by as I think about the turnstile, about my butt that now exists, and the want for the judgments to stop. But I do not know how to make them cease, how to allow myself space in my body in which to live. The sky slowly emerges from the quiet dark to a loud pink. I focus my eyes on the sky above the buildings and let the warm thoughts of what I have done to help my body rise in my mind. The bulimia has stopped. The cutting has stopped. The alcohol is now gone. My body tingles with pride at the steps I have made to get into this new version of myself. With these thoughts, I begin. Relax my legs, allow my skin to unhinge from its hyper-vigilance of the space I inhabit.

Ten hours later, on the train ride home, I release just a bit more into this new feeling. I practice the techniques of learning how to reside in my body. I allow my leg to touch the person next to me, to let her know I am a body that exists, that makes contact with the world. My polyester pants feel rough against my skin, the cloth pressing into my flesh as it nestles up against her gray skirt. When I enter my apartment, I strip my body of clothes, then slip into my pajamas. In the few seconds that exist between work clothes and pajamas, my body is naked to the world, my skin is caressed by the air and I am slowly welcoming my body back into myself. I carefully brush my teeth around the gums that have receded, and place my weary body into bed. I simply lie down and allow my body to rest, to slip into sleep.

BODY DREAMING

Chicago to Minneapolis, $60 round trip on Megabus. There is a writer, a woman who taught in Chicago this winter, who mentors me to get at my memories through writing. She teaches in Chicago, but lives in Minneapolis. We have started to become friends. I visit her monthly, take the eight-hour bus ride to get to the city that is beginning to feel like home. My body as it is encouraged by her, by writing, and by sobriety, also begins to feel like home, like a space in which I want to live.

I get on the bus at 10:30pm, and will arrive in Minneapolis at 6:30am. The bus floats into the night, the road underneath creating a steady, susurrating sound of *ssslllleeeeeeeeeeppp.* The tires glide, and I glide into tiredness, my body exhausted from the excitement of returning to the city with which I am slowly falling in love. Fatigued from trying to will the bus to go faster, I close my eyes against the moving world, and slip into my skin.

My head drifts back into the space it has known since I was a little kid in the car ride home from swim practice. I dream with my mind awake, fall into the desire of a body being hugged. And this time it is me who is doing the hugging. I want to hug, want to enter into the space in which I caress myself. So I practice the hugging on the bus, cross my arms tightly against my chest, my elbows slightly grazing those of the woman sitting in the seat next to me. I lean my head against the cool window, and daze into the image, into the feeling of me hugging me.

Minneapolis: My friend brings me to her apartment to nap before we head out to a coffee shop for the day. My body soaks into the brown leather couch, the place where I nap, where I sleep, where I claim as my own in her apartment. I close my eyes with a smile, continue the practice of hugging my arms around my body. It is my third trip there, and as my eyes slightly shut out the emerging pink morning light, I realize I have started to feel something different in me that I can't quite name.

It is a few days after my arrival and we host a party for two friends who are getting married the next fall. I stand in the bathroom, prepare my body for the party. The soft afternoon light reflects off of the mirror and hazes onto my skin. I slink my jeans off and pull my red dress out of my blue duffel bag. I have brought this dress and matching red heels for the occasion, but as I emerge from the bathroom with the red heels clunking on the floor, I realize I am unskilled at the art of walking female. My ankles wobble in the high heels, and keep tripping on the hard wooden floor as I try to plunk my way back to the living room to stash my belongings behind the brown couch. *This is ridiculous*. I cannot go through the night tripping over myself, cannot stand the thought of being so aware of my hips as they heave my weight from side to side, trying to balance the body that is not accustomed to sashaying this way, that is still learning how to claim the space of a female body with hips. On the couch, the brown leather suctions onto my almost bare thighs that poke out from the short, red dress, tear off the high heels and toss them back into my bag. I will go barefoot for the night, tromp around the floors in my cute red dress and bare soles.

Hours later, on the couch again, my body stripped of its dress and resting in green plaid boxers and a gray t-shirt. Everyone has left, and my drowsy body stretches along the length of the couch. The open window cools off my skin in the early summer heat. My back rests on the seat of the leather cushions. The crook of one elbow is over my forehead, and my right hand rests on my stomach. I feel dirt on my feet, and raise my right foot up to my hand to wipe it off. And that's when I notice it. The heel of my foot is dirty. Up until this point, I have been tiptoeing around myself, walking softly in order to feel light in my body, to not be noticed by the world. I have resisted the sound of myself walking, hoping to pass by people without them really seeing me.

The dark night hides my smile, but I can feel it there, can feel it spread across my face as I can just make out in the moonlight the evidence of something new, of the word that is slowly starting to emerge in my body. The dirt on my heels tells me I have been hitting the floor with all of my weight, with all of me. I have allowed my body to make noise, to exist. I smile wider at this shift. I do not wipe the dirt from myself, but instead extend my leg back down and think of the space in which I have finally arrived. I have moved back into the space of myself. And as I lie on the couch and consider this notion, the word enters into my head, whispers along my skin. *Home.* I can be at home in different cities, home in someone else's apartment, home on this couch that is not mine, because I am at home in my body. And it hits me, the realization that I can feel at home wherever I am because my home is with me is in my body is in me. My home is me.

BODYHOME

I have moved to Minneapolis, have moved into the space of myself, my home. It is night and I sit in a meditation AA meeting, opening up to the idea of faith and a higher power. My body rests on a creamy floral couch as I open up my senses to the idea of spirituality, to the feeling that there is something bigger than me in this life, that life is something of which I cannot control. My body is still, unmoving as if getting ready to sleep, and I feel my skin full with life, feel it vibrate with the involuntary wave of inhaling, exhaling. With my eyes closed, there is a glimpse of what I must do. I must let go of this body, allow it to take up whatever space it was meant to—no, *wants* to—inhabit. I must let go, and no longer try to control, to hide from myself. My body, like the world, is not mine to control, but is something for me to inhabit, to live.

I return home that night, enter my bedroom that I finally can claim as a space to live, the hard wooden floors softening my steps as I no longer resist their existence and coax my body out of its clothes. I remove my gray cotton shirt and strip away the layers of judgment. I begin to love the space of my body, my body as it is home to me. In the dark room, I hold my naked stomach. Now there is a stomach to hold. I grasp myself with compassion for my perceived imperfections. In the same way I do not resent the drips coming from the faucet, the way the pipes in my apartment growl with noise, the floorboards that creak under my weight, I love the home of my body for what it is: a home with flaws, with scars, with fat where there used to be negative space. And it is a cozy home, a soft home that provides comfort, a home in which I can live.

I furl my naked body back into the me-shaped dent in my bed. Curl into the body which is mine, my home. My body rests, turns off its conscious thoughts and curls up into the night. I close my eyes lightly to the world, and sink into my skin, relax my muscles in the shimmering moonlight. There are no longer other arms hugging me, or hands prying me apart. I have my scarred arms that are no longer scared, my steady hands with which to hold me. I smile into my mind, stroke the subtle rungs of my ribs, and take pride in the fact that I feel more skin, fat, and muscle than bone. My home is well insulated, my bodyhome here to keep the me inside of me. I roll over and expose the underbelly of my skin to the world. I open. I sleep. I dream. And when I wake up to the sight of my favorite color, the world at 4 a.m., I keep my mind in that space, the space of my body as my home, the space in which I desire to live.

Chelsey Clammer received her MA in Women's Studies from Loyola University Chicago, and is currently enrolled in the Rainier Writing Workshop MFA program. She has been published in *The Rumpus*, *Essay Daily*, and *The Water~Stone Review* among others. She is the Managing Editor and Nonfiction Editor for *The Doctor T.J. Eckleburg Review*, as well as a columnist and work-

shop instructor for the journal. She is also the Nonfiction Editor for *Pithead Chapel* and Associate Essays Editor for *The Nervous Breakdown*.

Aside from Pushcart and Best of the Net nominations, Clammer received an Honorary Mention for *Water~Stone Review*'s 2014 Judith Kitchen in Nonfiction Contest for her essay "A Striking Resemblance." Also in 2014, Clammer received 2nd place in *Black Warrior Review*'s nonfiction contest for her essay "Mother Tongue." Finally, she received *Minerva Rising*'s Owl of Minerva Award, 2014, a scholarship she used to take five young female recovering drug addicts with mental illness issues on a weekend writing retreat in a cabin in the Colorado Rocky Mountain Range.

Her second collection of essays, *There Is Nothing Else to See Here*, is forthcoming from The Lit Pub, Spring 2015. Clammer is working on a collection of essays, *Circadian*, that weaves scientific facts with personal stories in order to look at the poetics of the body.

www.chelseyclammer.com

CPSIA information can be obtained at www.ICGtesting.com
Printed in the USA
BVOW07s0103190215

388337BV00001B/3/P